It is impossible to control the environment around us. An overwhelmed parent cannot prevent the dog from barking, the kids from fighting, or a neighbor from ringing the doorbell. The student will always have to take exams. The policeman must face unknown danger, and the executive must continually deal with new responsibilities. But we can limit the ill effects of stress by taking control of the environment within ourselves and of our own reactions to stressful situations. Stress is not caused by the environment outside ourselves. Stress is the result of our *reaction* to the outer environment.

Also Published by Ballantine Books:

THE THOUGHT-A-WEEK GUIDES: HOW TO BE A BETTER PARENT

THE THOUGHT-A-WEEK GUIDES: HOW TO HAVE A BETTER RELATIONSHIP

THE THOUGHT A WEEK GUIDES: HOW TO COPE WITH STRESS

A Blue Cliff Editions Book

Catherine Cianci Karas

BALLANTINE BOOKS • NEW YORK

Library of Congress Catalog Card Number: 86-91597

ISBN 0-345-33341-1

Printed in Canada

First Edition: March 1987

To Dimitri and Christina for their enduring patience.

ACKNOWLEDGMENTS

My heartfelt appreciation goes to all those who helped in their own ways to make this book possible. First to my parents, Phil and Florence Cianci, who always made my education a high priority. Next, to my many teachers, who guided me along the way, with a special thanks to the late Eva Pierrakos for her lectures. To Jason Shulman for his inspiration, and to Arlene Shulman for her solid support during the dark moments.

INTRODUCTION

What is stress? We all have our own personal conceptions of what stress is to us. For a parent, it may be trying to cook dinner while the children are fighting, the doorbell is ringing, the dog is barking, and a pot is boiling over. For a student, it may be the pressure of a final exam. For a policeman, it could be the stress of unexpected danger on the job, and for an executive, it may be the stress of coordinating many tasks simultaneously. Although the causes of people's feelings of stress are often quite different, one thing is certain: We must all deal with stress at one time or another.

Some stress is good for us. It gets us going and lends a certain degree of excitement to our lives. But chronic stress can be deadly. It saps energy, wastes time, and can threaten health and even life. Stress can make us uncomfortable—with tense muscles and headaches, with knots in our stomach, cold, clammy hands, or a blank mind. At its worst, stress can even kill, by promoting heart attacks and strokes. People experience many different psychosomatic reactions to stress, including ulcers, migraine headaches, back pain, colitis, and nervous tics. Certainly, no one enjoys living with chronic stress, yet many of us do not know how to limit it.

It is impossible to control the environment around us. An overwhelmed parent cannot prevent the dog from barking, the kids from fighting, or a neighbor from ringing the doorbell. The student will always have to take exams. The policeman must face unknown dangers, and the executive must continually deal with new responsibilities. But we can limit the ill effects of stress by taking control of our own reactions to stressful situations. Stress is not caused by the environment outside ourselves. Stress is the result of our *reactions* to the outer environment.

This book will help you take charge of your own reactions to stressful situations. By learning about your body, mind, emotions, management skills, and personal habits, you will become more aware of your own responses. When you can cope with and modify your own reactions to stressful stimuli, you will experience less stress. By using the thoughts for each week as guidelines in your daily life, you will find that stress is something you can work on and reduce, and thereby increase the pleasure in your life.

Some stress is beneficial, too much hurts.

Donald is a very busy man. He runs his own small manufacturing business on a shoestring with a minimum of help. Finances are tight and business varies greatly from month to month, so he never really knows what to expect.

Donald always feels as if he is in a rush. He rushes in the morning to get to work, he hurries around the office trying to complete calls and paperwork, he pushes his employees to get the product out and delivered, he runs to meetings with customers, and at the end of the day he feels burdened and bushed.

Because Donald always feels in such a hurry, he never feels comfortable taking the time to organize and take charge of his situation. As a result, he often misses important calls or appointments, and spends unnecessary time looking for things he has misplaced. Much of the time he feels confused and overwhelmed.

Donald runs around with knots in his stomach. Because of his chaotic situation, he always feels a sense of urgency about his work. Everything seems to threaten the life of the business, and his body responds as if he were in actual physical danger, pumping adrenaline throughout his system.

This reaction to stress, the pumping of adrenaline through the body, has been called the "fight or flight" response. This week we are going to become familiar with the fight or flight response in ourselves and observe how we use or abuse it.

The fight or flight response is an important way for the body to adapt to a sudden change. It is part of our survival system, allowing us to function very effectively in alarming situations. When we call upon this response, adrenaline, a potent hormone, is released. It affects the entire body: The pulse and blood pressure increase; the central nervous system is stimulated; digestion is suspended, allowing more blood to supply the muscles for quick action; blood-clotting ability increases; and blood sugar increases. Such physical readiness is essential for us when we are in real danger and unnecessary when we aren't. The problem for someone like Donald is that he sustains a feeling of danger in his life and therefore calls forth the fight or flight response regularly. This has detrimental effects on his body.

The stress created by living in a state of fight or flight readiness wears down the body until eventually the weakest system breaks down and illness occurs, such as headaches, heart disease, high blood pressure, ulcers, colitis, kidney ailments, and impotence. The state of illness creates more stress, which in turn produces more illness, and you find yourself in a vicious circle of stress and illness.

People live in a high and constant state of stress for various reasons. Some don't realize that there is an alternative. For them, life has always felt stressful. Others are motivated by the exciting feeling of adrenaline coursing through the body. It feels good to them to have that rush, and they feel let down without it. Others simply haven't realized what it is they do that increases their stress. Each type of person has a great deal to gain by altering the pattern of living in order to decrease the stress level.

Chronic stress becomes distress. Positive stress, on the other hand, helps to motivate us toward our goals. We all need some stress to keep us going. The tricky part is to find the balance between enough stress and too much stress. Donald is an obvious example of someone who lives with too much stress too often. He lives in a state of distress. You can, if you want to, find the right amount of stress for you and live in a state of positive stress.

Positive stress is the edge of anxiety we feel when we are going to perform. It perks us up and gives up that little bit of extra attentiveness we need to do our best. We may feel it when we are about to take a test, speak in front of others, perform, or do anything about which we feel a bit unsure. This extra bit of adrenaline helps us. Too much adrenaline for too long a time hurts us.

This week observe your fight or flight response. You can recognize it as the way you feel when you are truly frightened: racing heart, butterflies in the stomach, knot in the throat, sweating, short rapid breathing, irritability. It may not always feel that intense, but you will feel that heightened sensibility to a degree. Get a feeling for how much time you spend in that state.

Does it feel excessive to your situation? Is it more than you want or need? Ask yourself whether it really gives you anything positive. Do you have distress or positive stress? Choose the right amount of stress for yourself this week, and work toward building the balance you need.

I acknowledge my limitations.

Much of our stress is generated by fighting things that cannot be changed. It is easy to build up steam about the injustices and absurdities we see in the world around us. Certainly there are many things in the world that need to be changed. But where does our frustration get us? Does it accomplish anything? Usually not, unless we distinguish what we can change from what we cannot.

This week when you find a situation that you think needs to be changed, ask yourself, "Can this situation be changed?" If you determine that it can, then ask yourself, "What do I have to do to effect a change for the better?" Then ask yourself, "Am I prepared to do what is required to make this change?" If you are—wonderful. Set your goal, draw up a plan, and take action. If you're not prepared to institute the change, or if circumstances make change impossible, simply recognize this fact and try to let go of your frustration.

There are only two effective alternatives: Do something about the problem, or recognize that you cannot or will not effect a change and let it go. Any other approach is a waste of energy and will result in stress. Nothing increases stress more than feelings of helplessness—and that's exactly what is created when we want something changed but feel powerless to accomplish it. If you're not willing or able to change something, accept this fact and save yourself from unproductive and needless anxiety. Try to forgive yourself for the limitations that prevent you from changing it, let go of your frustration, and give yourself some peace of mind.

I take time for a break.

One simple way to deal with anger or upset is to count to ten before you respond to a situation. Here is an expanded version of that old-fashioned method. It is a technique for concentration that can help to center us when things become too much for us to take.

Taking the time to ease your mind through concentration can help lower your blood pressure. It has even been known to replace medication for some people—of course, only with the guidance of their physicians. But most important, perhaps, it can give you a break from stress and allow you to find the inner space to cope with the events at hand. Best of all, regular concentration can help you feel very relaxed.

The technique is really very simple.

First sit or lie in as comfortable a position as you can. Close your eyes. Be as quiet as possible. Pay attention to your breathing. Notice the air moving in and out of your lungs. Do not change your breathing, just notice it. Begin to count your breaths in groups of four, with each complete breath (inhalation and exhalation) counting as one. As you inhale and exhale, count one; with the next breath, count two; and so on with the third and fourth breaths. With the fifth breath, begin the sequence again. As you are doing this simple activity, you will notice that your mind will intrude with its own agenda: "Why did Jane seem so distant last night?" or "What can I serve for dinner on Thursday?" or "That last memo from Joe really bothered me," and so on. This reaction is natural, but it minimizes the effectiveness of the exercise. So when you're aware that your thoughts are intruding, gently guide all your attention back to counting your breaths. Every time you are aware of your mind's wandering, bring it back to your breathing again. You may also experience some anxiety as you become acquainted with the quietness of your mind. Simply treat this just as you would a thought—that is, by concentrating on your breathing again.

That's all there is to it. It's simple but not really easy. Begin by concentrating for five minutes and slowly build up to twenty minutes at a time. Some people find this kind of concentration so helpful that they do it regularly for twenty minutes in the morning and twenty minutes in the evening—*before* they feel overwhelmed. Remember, do not try to achieve perfection or look for immediate results. This will only create strain and tension. The effectiveness of your concentration will vary from day to day, depending on your state of mind. But with practice, it will become easier to concentrate. This week experiment with this method of concentration. It may be your doorway to inner peace and relaxation. Do what works well for you.

I create clarity through goal setting.

Living your life without conscious goals is like trying to draw in the dark. You can see neither what you've done nor what needs to be done, and the result is likely to be an indecipherable mess.

Life without clear-cut, conscious goals is stressful because you have no indication of where you're going or how you're doing. And without ways of evaluating your efforts, it is difficult to be efficient, make changes in the way you live, and, most important, feel good about yourself and the job you're doing. The result is an aimless, fuzzy, frustrating feeling about your life.

What actually happens is that your life is directed by unconscious goals. The unconscious mind will fulfill the role of the goal setter in the absence of the conscious goal setter. This is a dangerous situation, as the unconscious mind works in immature and hidden ways that are often ill motivated. Its goals may be spiteful, vengeful, and destructive rather than creative and constructive. It is not a good way to achieve a rewarding and fulfilling life.

Having clear and conscious goals, on the other hand, helps you keep moving in a forward direction and makes it simple for you to know where you're going and how you're doing. For example, if you have decided that by the age of thirty you want to be six years into your career, married two years, and own your own home, it is easy for you to chart your progress toward your goals. By making an assessment, you can determine which goals have been achieved and how close you are to achieving the others. This will show you where to focus your attention.

You may decide that you need to intensify your efforts in a particular area, or on the contrary, you may decide that your goal was overambitious and knowing what you know now you can modify it. In either case, you have good, clear feedback about where you are and how you're doing. If it does nothing else, goal setting and goal reviewing makes you take a look at what is happening in your life in a specific context.

Bob and Fran are a very goal-directed couple. They are both successful in their careers and have similar goals for family life. Last year they decided that they wanted to re-locate and Bob wanted a change of job. They set the goal: Bob would find a new job, and they would find a new home in a new location within twelve to eighteen months.

Bob immediately sent out résumés. Within fourteen months Bob had landed a better job in a new location in an area they both preferred, and they had sold their co-op apartment and bought a new house near Bob's job.

If after eighteen months nothing had changed, they would then have needed to examine the situation, see where they had to take action, or possibly revise their goals. They had guidelines for evaluating what was happening.

Bob and Fran are good examples of how goal setting gets things moving and keeps you on track.

Now evaluate realistically how you might reach a goal. How would you do it? What are the real costs (time, energy, money, sacrifices)? How long would it take? Are you willing to give what it takes to attain the goal, or do you want to modify the goal?

This week choose one area of your life in which to set goals. It could be in the area of your career, your family or social life, your financial or vocational plans, or your spiritual growth. Think about your hopes and dreams for that aspect of your life. Allow yourself to reach for your fondest dreams.

I use affirmations to change my life.

Have there ever been areas in your life that despite everything you try, you seem powerless to change? Have you felt frustrated and helpless because of them? There is a potent way of dealing with these resistant areas of our lives—using affirmations.

Affirmations are a way of literally changing one's mind. They are positive statements of what we want to be that replace what has been previously programmed in our minds.

For example, Sally has been trying very hard to make a profit in her dress shop. She has studied all the right courses, taken all the right steps, employs good salespeople, and yet never seems to do better than just break even. Making a profit would mean success to Sally. Yet in her mind her brother Tim is the successful one, she is the one who can just get by. After all, that's how it always was in school, wasn't it?

Sally struggles with the belief that the best she can do is just get by. Intellectually, she understands this is not the truth, but her emotions are attached to that belief. Consequently, in subtle ways, Sally sabotages her attempts at success.

Sally could use affirmations to alter her mistaken belief. For example, she might state the way she would really like to be: "I am a successful businesswoman with a profitable business." By reaffirming this thought in her mind again and again, Sally can change her belief about herself.

Each one of us has areas in our lives where we are stymied by unconscious counterproductive beliefs.

This week we will use affirmations to change these beliefs and enhance our lives.

For the first day review your life and identify the areas that are the most difficult for you. Choose one particular problem area to work with this week.

Write an affirmation to change this life area. Imagine what would make this situation perfect for you. Make a concise statement that reflects this perfect circumstance in the present tense. Leave it open-ended, state it positively (use no negatives), and make sure that it is at no one's expense.

For example, Sally's affirmation, "I am a successful businesswoman with a profitable business" is in the first person (I), present tense (am), all in positive terms, and is at no one's expense. An ineffective affirmation for Sally to use would be, "I will be a more successful businesswoman than Jane, and I won't have any debts." This is in the future tense (will be), it is at Jane's expense (than Jane), and it contains negatives (won't).

Another example of an effective affirmation is: I am in a happy and fulfilling marriage. It is effective because it is in the present tense (am), it is at no one's expense, and it contains no negatives.

An ineffective version would be, I want to be married to Ted's wife and want to live happily ever after. This is obviously at Ted's expense and in the future tense.

For the rest of the week use your affirmation. Every day as you read or say your affirmation, feel as if you are already experiencing this perfect situation. Repeat the affirmation as often as you feel comfortable over the next seven days. Afterward, feel appreciation for what you have received as if you had already received it.

Make sure to include this step and be patient with yourself until your emotions are able to catch up to the affirmation. Notice how you feel after doing the affirmations. You will probably feel more positive and more fulfilled, which in turn will help you to manifest your affirmation in your life.

Try using affirmations to make your life what you want it to be. You deserve it!

Disorder causes stress.

Things in disorder are stressful. They create a sense of loss of control that can be threatening.

Most of us do not like the feeling of being out of control, especially about events in our lives. This situation creates anxiety, stress, confusion, and frustration. And yet so often we refuse to take the steps necessary to create order and relieve the stress.

There are many reasons for our resistance to taking corrective action. We all have our own, but common ones are: rebelling against a strict upbringing, in which neatness and order were emphasized; dislike of maintenance tasks; and indolence.

Although resistance may be used as an excuse for not keeping one's house in order, it does not excuse the related stress.

For example, Ned wanted to reduce his stress level; yet it never seemed to diminish. Ned took pride in his ability to juggle his life without much structure. He had papers all over his desk, couldn't find his telephone in the chaos in his apartment, and often forgot appointments and phone calls. He felt as if he were defeating the odds each time something in his life worked out well and on time. It seemed as if Ned had to prove to himself over and over again how capable he was by working against the difficulties he put in front of himself.

Ned paid a big price for this. His colleagues viewed him skeptically, and they became doubtful about his capabilities. As a result, they underestimated his true abilities and bypassed him for career moves. His colleagues' actions frustrated him, and he became stressed and agitated. Gradually he slept poorly and lost his appetite.

Finally Ned stopped trying to play hero and started to order his environment. He found that he functioned so much better that his true abilities were evident and he no longer had to prove himself. His friends and colleagues gained respect for him, and he gained respect for himself.

This week take stock of your life. In which areas do you have disorder? Is your home neat and orderly? Do you know where things are? Is it easy to get to them and put them back?

How is your work space? Do you know where things are, and can you find them easily? Is it organized efficiently?

Each of us has areas we can organize better. Spend the first two days this week thinking about which areas to tidy up. For the next two days, make a plan about how to reorganize them, and for the last three days, implement your plan.

For example, your linen closet might be out of control. You may not know where to find a washcloth or a pillowcase that matches your sheets. Take the time to clean out the closet and reorganize it. It is helpful to label each shelf with tags reminding you what goes where, so that when you put things back, it is easier to keep order. After you have done this, it should be a pleasure to use your closet, and you will be ready to tackle even greater organizational tasks in your life.

Make some order out of chaos this week, and enjoy the clarity.

I let go of attachments.

We are born of attachment. We die attached. We live a life of attachments. Yet holding on to attachments is often stressful. We are attached to our family, our friends, our ideas, our possessions, and our identities—even to getting our own way.

Letting go of attachments is an important way to reduce stress. Life is full of comings-together and goings-apart, a dance of separation and unity. If we can flow with the rhythm of the dance, we enjoy it. If we fight the flow of the movement, we suffer.

We fight the flow of the dance when we won't accept things the way they are. We need to find peace in the reality of the moment, letting things be. That does not mean that we cannot want things to be different but rather that we do not demand that they be different. Only by accepting reality are we able to live truly in the moment.

We need to be able to let go in the middle of an argument when it is clear it's not going to be resolved. We need to be able to let go of a loved one when she's gone, and then, eventually, let go of the pain and sadness of that loss. We need to be able to let go of our ideas, temporarily, no matter how good, if the time is not right. Sometimes we need to let go of fixed beliefs just because not everything in life is fixed and rigid. And we need to let go of the idea that we always know what in life is best for us.

This week we are going to observe our attachments and practice letting go of some of them.

For the first three days, notice moments when you feel anxious or stressed. Ask yourself whether you are, at that moment, holding onto an attachment. Are you not getting your way? Did you lose something or someone of importance to you? Did you experience a loss of face? Notice what kinds of attachments are strongest for you.

For the next four days, when you feel stressed by the loss of an attachment, gently talk yourself into letting go of that attachment. Be gentle and kind, accepting your reaction to your loss. Be supportive and understanding. And let your attachment go. If you have a demand that someone do something, ask yourself how important it really is if he or she does it or not. What would happen if that person didn't? How could you handle that? Ask yourself what is more important, your peace of mind or having the person accede to your demands?

How does it feel letting go in the middle of a dispute? Do you feel relieved? Less stressed? Do you feel defeated? If so, you are holding on to the concept of winning or losing. Let go of that, and simply allow yourself to feel good about keeping your equanimity.

If you are attached to things being a certain way, ask yourself how important it really is. What about the present reality is so terrible? How can you accept it and feel better? Much of our stress arises from demanding life be a certain way rather than simply dealing with it as it is.

Let go of some attachments this week. You'll dance better for it.

I lose myself in a hobby.

"The world is too much with us," the poet Wordsworth tells us. And we know that, too. We know that there are times when we want to stop what is going on around us and forget about it. Although it is important and necessary for us to be self-aware and aware of our responsibilities, it is equally important to have time when we can have the luxury of forgetting ourselves and our responsibilities. This week we are going to explore the luxury of losing ourselves in a hobby as a way of reducing the stress of feeling constantly responsible.

We live in a culture in which maximum productivity is given high value. Consequently, we often denigrate activities that are not immediately productive. This is an attitude to challenge.

We have all heard that "All work and no play makes Jack a dull boy." This is true, because Jack has run himself down with too much concentration on getting his work out and not enough attention to taking care of his need for play.

Relaxing with a hobby is regenerating. We can become so absorbed in our hobbies that we are able to forget our responsibilities and problems and can let go and feel free

21

for a while. It is time free of encumbrances, free from external demands, free from everything except the pleasure of our hobbies.

And after we have relaxed with our hobbies, we are able to be more creative and productive in our work.

Many of us have not yet discovered what hobbies most captivate us. Others of us have. This week those of us in the first group will find hobbies, and those of us in the second group will spend time with hobbies we already have.

The first group will find hobbies in which they can truly lose themselves. One way of doing this is to think back to your childhood and remember the activities that captured you back then, when you were more spontaneous. Did you like making models? Growing plants? Drawing? Baking? Participating in sports? Singing? Dancing? Collecting things? Sculpting? Reading about a particular subject? Painting? Spend some time thinking about what hobby from your childhood still appeals to you today.

If you have a hard time remembering what you loved to do as a child, then think about those things that you've found interesting as an adult. There must be activities that you've thought of doing "someday when I've got the time."

Another source of ideas for hobbies is adult education classes. Most communities have courses for adults, and many of these courses can be hobbies.

Take the time you need this week to identify a hobby you want to try. Get the materials you need for it or sign up for a class. Remember, this is supposed to be fun, not work, so go at it lightly with the idea of enjoying yourself. If you find that it starts to feel like a burden, you've found the wrong hobby.

Now, once you've found a hobby, and for those of you who already have a hobby, find at least two hours this week to devote yourself completely to your hobby. You may find it so much fun and so refreshing that you will continue it regularly.

Lose yourself in a hobby. Enjoy.

I accept my imperfections.

One way we load ourselves with unnecessary stress is by expecting ourselves to be perfect. We become unrealistic about our limitations and place unreasonably high expectations on ourselves. Clearly, this is a way to create disappointment and disillusionment, leaving us feeling pressured to do more and do better.

Yet, acknowledging to ourselves or to others that we are fallible can be quite difficult. We often need to swallow our pride in order to do so. But the very act of swallowing our pride can be a tremendous relief. We no longer have to hold up the image that we are perfect. We no longer have to strive to hide our errors. We no longer have to pretend that we are who we are not.

Protecting this image of being who we are not is what causes the stress. We live in constant fear of being found out and exposed. We work hard to cover our tracks and maintain our images. We're afraid to let our guard down and be ourselves, lest someone finds out who we really are.

Most of us have expectations of ourselves, but it is the degree to which we try to live up to those false expectations that causes the stress. The more we invest in our image of being a perfect person, the more stress it causes us.

This week we will observe how much we invest in our perfectionism and take steps to decrease that investment.

For the first three days, observe yourself when you make mistakes. Do you accept them as part of life, nothing particularly important? Or do you stop short, and become paralyzed? Do you feel embarrassed? Humiliated? Frightened? Angry? Do you forgive yourself easily for making mistakes, or do you berate yourself and put yourself down? Do you hide your errors, or can you expose them with equanimity?

For the last four days, take steps to help yourself accept the fact that you are not perfect. Try being honest with yourself and others about your errors. Acknowledge to others, especially those close to you, when you are in error. Take responsibility for your mistakes. Be ready to say I'm sorry, if it is appropriate.

Then forgive yourself for your mistakes. Don't judge yourself, put yourself down, or dwell on how it could have been. Accept the simple fact that you made an error and take responsibility for the consequences. This may mean facing people who make you uncomfortable, paying a monetary or emotional price, cleaning up and correcting the mistake, or doing whatever is necessary to make restitution for the error.

Accept your imperfections this week. You'll be stronger for it!

I pay attention to my needs.

Like it or not, we all have needs. We have physical needs, safety needs, social needs, and needs for esteem. Many of our needs are met, but some remain unmet. It is the chronically unmet needs in our lives that cause stress.

When we constantly ignore certain needs, symptoms of stress can develop. These resulting symptoms may be physical, emotional, or mental. For example, too little sleep leaves us tired, irritable, mentally cloudy, and unpleasant to be with. Insufficient time alone may leave us simply irritable. The symptom is a signal from you to yourself that some need is being ignored.

It is interesting to note that people often believe that ignoring their own needs is in some way noble. This may be from the notion that we should put others first. While it is important to think of others, we first need to take care of ourselves. We must keep ourselves healthy and in top shape so that we will be able to take care of our other responsibilities.

Recognizing our own needs may be tricky at first, especially if we have become accustomed to ignoring them. By thinking of broad categories of needs, however, we can get an overview of typical needs and compare them to our own. Some needs to be aware of are: physical needs (food, sleep, exercise, touching, sex), security needs (shelter, financial resources, supportive people), social needs (loved ones, friends), vocational needs (some purpose for living one's life), and emotional and spiritual needs (love, sense of connectedness to something bigger than oneself, self-esteem, respect from others, connectedness to one's deeper self, time alone).

In order to discover our needs, it is helpful to recognize how we disguise them. We can deny them by saying they don't exist. We can project them onto others seeing them in everyone else but not in ourselves. And we can judge them, making them seem unimportant. These defenses against needs keep them out of mind and keep them unfulfilled.

This week spend the first three days observing yourself for symptoms of unfilled needs. Are you cranky when you are around other people but perfectly at peace when you are alone? Then you may need more time to yourself. Are you sleepy, mentally foggy, and irritable? Then you may need more sleep. Are you feeling achy, gaining weight, and losing flexibility in your body? Then you may need to eat better and exercise more.

Pay attention to any physical, mental, or emotional disharmony. This is a sign from you to yourself that something needs attention. This is your red flag saying, "Stop, look, and listen. Danger ahead."

From these first days of observation, identify two or three needs you have been ignoring. For the next four days, make and implement a plan to take care of filling those needs. For example, you may discover that you need more physical touching. Plan to ask a friend, relative, or mate for hugs and touching each day. If that feels too hard to do, touch yourself.

At the end of the week, see how you feel about asking for and getting those needs met. Do you feel better? Have the symptoms been lessened?

Get your needs met this week. You'll feel better for it!

I can say no.

Each one of us has at some time felt the need to please someone. In our childhood, it was important to please our parents, teachers, and other authorities. As adults, we try to please our mates, our bosses, our clients, our friends. Pleasing others has become a habit, an automatic and immediate response in many situations.

There is nothing inherently stressful about pleasing others. Stress arises, however, when we please others instead of ourselves. Unfortunately, many of us don't recognize when we are pleasing others at our own expense.

Adam is a good example. Adam is a young executive. He is single and has devoted his life to advancing his career. He is personable and agreeable but occasionally inexplicably angry.

Adam mistakenly believes that the way to the top is to be a yes man. He agrees with anything that his superiors in the office hierarchy say. This means that he takes on any work, any blame, any criticism, and agrees with it. Inevitably, there are times when Adam can't produce more work, isn't truly to blame, and doesn't warrant the criticism. Yet he accepts it.

The result for Adam is a well of unexpressed anger that floods out "inexplicably" at his subordinates.

What Adam, and all of us, needs is the courage and conviction to say no. We need to accept the risk and consequences of saying no to someone whose favor we desire. We need to say no to those who have power over us. And we need to say no to those we love and who love us.

Saying no can be a tremendously liberating experience. We no longer carry the burden of our unspoken no, and therefore we don't create anger resulting from self-betrayal. Additionally, we are saying yes to ourselves, and giving ourselves the freedom of our courage and convictions.

Initially, saying no when we're afraid to say no does create some anxiety. This is probably unavoidable, the price we must pay for changing old patterns. The payoff, however, is great, as we develop our ability to assert our true convictions and increase our self-esteem.

This week spend the first three days noticing in which situations you are likely to say yes when you'd want to say no. To whom do you tend to sell out? Pinpoint the kinds of situations that lend themselves easily to your self-betrayal. Make notes for future reference.

For the last four days, take your courage in hand and once each day say no to someone to whom you'd usually say yes.

How does this feel? Do you feel stronger, having said no? Do you feel more self-confident? Do you feel freer? Less angry? Do you have more self-esteem?

After these four days, you will feel much less stressed.

Feel freer this week. Say no to someone.

I decrease body tension.

Are you tense? You probably think so, or you wouldn't be reading this book! We know we are tense by feeling tightness or discomfort in our bodies. This week, we are going to deal directly with a symptom of stress—body tension. It is possible to decrease body tension directly without dealing with the underlying issues. This, of course, is not a panacea, but it will help to get you through those times when there's time to do only a quick fix-up.

In order to decrease body tension, it is essential that you be able to identify the tense areas. To do this, scan your body from the head down or from the feet up. Go slowly through each body segment to determine the degree of tension. Note any area that is very tense. When you have finished, go back to the tense areas. Stay with each one a while and familiarize yourself with it. That means describing it to yourself. What color is it? What shape is it? What are its dimensions? If it could speak, what would it say?

Once you feel as if you have gotten to know the tense area, see it in your mind's eye and watch it begin to melt. It may melt into the same color it was originally, or the color may change. The shape will change. Allow the tense area to continue melting, and see the river of melted tension flow down and out of your body. For example, if you have a red headache, you may envision a red river flowing down your back, legs, and out your feet. As this happens, the tension should lessen.

If this method does not work well for you, or if you are pressed for time, there is a simpler way to relieve muscular tension. Again, locate the areas of tension. Contract those muscles so they are as tight as possible. Hold tight for a count of six, then suddenly release the muscle and relax. This increases the amount of relaxation almost immediately. If you are unsure of how to tighten the tense muscle, simply exaggerate the tension you feel. This is particularly helpful for people with sedentary jobs who develop tension in their shoulders. By lifting the shoulders as high as possible for a count of six and then suddenly letting them drop, they can relax those muscles. Follow this with five very deep breaths that fill your entire trunk.

This week familiarize yourself with your body, particularly your tense areas. Get to know how they feel when they are tense and when they are relaxed. At least once each day, scan your body for tension. Learn how to release the tension quickly and effectively. Take the time to relax whenever you notice tension.

Decrease body tension this week. You'll enjoy the feeling.

I put my priorities in order.

It is likely that at some time this week you will find yourself in a cloud of confusion. There will be outside pressures, personal needs, and responsibilities all crying for attention at the same time.

A common response to this situation is to feel confused. You don't know which way to turn. You begin to feel ineffectual and helpless. At times it feels as if a fog has descended and clouded your thinking.

This is threatening to you; you feel yourself losing control. The flight or fight mechanism is alerted and you become stressed.

As a school administrator, Greg would often find himself overwhelmed with duties. He was responsible for supervising the administrative personnel and the teachers, overseeing the students, and keeping the parents informed and satisfied.

One day he found himself with too many things to do and not enough time to do them. There were reports to write, students to discipline, teachers' meetings, and parents to see. It was obvious that Greg couldn't do all of these things and do them well.

At the point when Greg was feeling most agitated and

disorganized, overwhelmed and ineffectual, he took one simple step and changed it all: Greg stopped, looked carefully at each thing he had to do, and gave it a number that rated its importance. By the time he had finished, Greg knew what he was going to do first. He felt organized, in control, and effectual. He still had too little time to do everything, but at least he now knew how he was going to proceed.

This simple technique can help you at any time. It helps before you are overwhelmed and afterward as well. Some people wouldn't think of starting their day without deciding what was most important for them to do. Listing your priorities saves you from making decisions about them over and over. Once you have ordered them, you know what to attend to next.

This week try listing your priorities. Sit down, take a couple of deep breaths, and write down everything you have to do on that day. Now take another couple of deep breaths and ask yourself, "What is the most important thing I have to do?" Label that number one. Then figure out the next most important thing to do and label that number two. Continue until every item on your list is numbered.

Now don't drive yourself crazy trying to be precise. What is important here is a general order to the flow of your day, not the accuracy of your list. It is possible to get so caught up in making the list exactly right that you get nothing done the whole day. Obviously this is not the point.

This is helpful not only to people who have too much to do, but also for people who have a lot of unstructured time. That can cause as much anxiety as too little time. When people feel that they have all the time in the world to do things, they often get very little done and find themselves feeling undirected and hazy. By creating a structure, by ordering their priorities, they can create order and a sense of accomplishment.

If lists intimidate you, take heart: You are not alone. Many people are afraid of them. See them for what they are, tools to help create order, rather than monsters that control you. Remember, you are in charge of your list, rather than your list being in charge of you. If, in the middle of following your list, you decide that it is not for you, you always have the option of tearing it up and throwing it away, and you are no worse off than when you began.

Put your priorities in order this week. It will help reduce your stress.

The time I spend alone
is time well spent.

Do you ever feel as if you've lost touch with yourself, your deepest hopes and dreams, your deepest desires and feelings? At times we all lose touch with our deepest selves. Keeping the communication with our deeper selves alive requires time and attention. It is stressful to lose contact with our inner selves, our truest selves, because we become directed by the outer circumstances in our lives rather than by our inner voice. When we do, we stray from ourselves, creating conflict between who we think we should be (as defined by outer circumstances) and who we truly are.

One way to keep this conflict to a minimum is by spending time alone. Time alone allows for the possibility of communication with our inner selves. It creates a time in which we are protected from outer demands, a time in which we can be totally attuned to our needs, desires, and wishes. This time can be deeply satisfying and replenishing.

One reason we resist giving ourselves time alone is that we are afraid that if there's not someone else with us, we will feel empty and anxious.

It is important to remember that we are actually quite complete in ourselves, and in fact, we may be our own best company, if we only give ourselves the time and space to discover our inner selves. It may be difficult to get through those first minutes, maybe even hours by ourselves, but once you've traversed them, you may find a tranquility and a serenity you have yearned for.

This time alone can be used in whatever way you want. You may want to watch TV, read, listen to music, think, write, play games, do relaxation exercises, physical exercises, make plans, organize, clean up odds and ends— whatever you are moved to do. This is time just for you. Give yourself the freedom to be yourself, following your impulses. By allowing yourself to go in any direction you want, you'll learn to know yourself better. Over the week you may find the quality of your time alone changing. This will give you an opportunity to have more connection with your deeper self.

This week notice how much time you have alone, truly alone. Then map out some time to spend alone, undisturbed. It can be one half hour each day, or three hours at once. The most important thing is that you are able to work it comfortably into your schedule.

Notice what you do with your time. How do you feel during your time alone? How do you feel afterward? How do you feel about being with other people before and after your time alone? Do you know yourself better afterward? Have you found more communication with your deeper self? Is there some way you can reach yourself more deeply while you're alone?

Get to know yourself better this week. Spend some time alone!

I give myself enough time.

□

Do you ever feel as if you have enough time? It is a luxurious feeling! One way we stress ourselves is to plan (or not plan) our lives so that we have unrealistic demands on our time. You may find your body pumping adrenaline into your bloodstream simply because you're running late. For most people, lateness is an important cause of stress, because it is a problem that recurs throughout each day. You may be subjecting your nervous system to many unnecessary alterations and putting yourself on alert for emergency action when it is really unwarranted. This creates much unnecessary wear and tear on your body.

For example, suppose it takes you twenty minutes door-to-door to reach your office—that is, if

1. The buses are running on schedule,
2. There are no traffic jams,
3. The telephone doesn't ring as you are going out the door, and
4. You don't stop to talk to anyone on the street or stop to do an errand before work.

So it takes you twenty minutes to get to work if everything works together unimpeded. If you leave home twenty minutes before you need to be at work, you will invariably worry about lateness all the way to work. It may give you a charge, but all that tension also raises your anxiety level for those twenty minutes and puts you on edge. You may be paying too high a price for the excitement of discovering whether you can beat the clock.

The remedy for your situation is simple: Leave the house a half hour before you need to be at work. The payoff is great. You'll be more relaxed, so you can enjoy your trip to work. You don't need to worry about traffic or other things that are beyond your control. Besides, it's great to sit on the bus and be able to become absorbed in a book rather than chewing your nails down to the quick.

For the first half of this week, take stock of the way you budget your time. Do you leave enough time to get where you're going easily? Do you allow enough time to complete your tasks thoroughly and carefully? Keep track of the way you handle your time. Get an idea of how close you are to making things easier for yourself. Do you need to just allow ten minutes here and there, or do you really have to make major revisions in the way you plan your time?

For the remainder of the week, make the necessary adjustments in your schedule and habits so that you can reduce this stress in your daily life. How do you feel when you allow yourself plenty of time to do what you need to do? Do you like this new way of feeling, or did you like it better the old way?

— You may want to continue with your new, reduced stress schedule on an ongoing basis. You will be rewarded with less stress and more energy.

I unclutter my mind.

One way we create tension and stress is by carrying around mental notes. We have to keep track of birthdays, appointments, groceries, errands, changes of schedules, and endless numbers of other details of our lives. We often forget some of these things, and we fear forgetting others. A lot of mental energy is expended holding on to and keeping these mental lists straight.

Some of this is, of course, necessary. But an excess creates unnecessary stress. This week we are going to observe our styles of dealing with life's details and use an exercise to free our minds from this trivia.

For the first three days, observe yourself and see how you coordinate your mental notes. Are you efficient, forgetting only a few things? Do you have difficulty keeping track of them? Are you superassiduous, never forgetting any of them? Do you worry that you are forgetting something? Do you have an internal monitor that alerts you when you have forgotten something? Are you relaxed about your attention to details? After these three days, you will have an idea how much stress is generated by these mental notes.

For the last four days, we will relieve our minds of

having to carry around all this information. It is really quite simple. Buy a small pad of paper that you can keep with you at all times. Some are small enough to fit into the pocket of a shirt. Have a pen or pencil available, too. When you think of something you have to remember or something you need to do, write it down. Get it out of your mind and relieve yourself of the stress of trying to remember it.

Of course there is one more thing to remember: to look at the pad periodically. Don't forget to refer to the list occasionally to keep up to date and cross things off as they are done. By being conscientious about writing things down as they occur to you, you will be better organized and less anxious about forgetting things. Your mind will have the freedom to be more creative and you will feel more secure.

Use a notepad this week and unclutter your mind!

I choose whom to trust.

□

Many of us inadvertently add to our stress by confiding in the wrong people. Some people can help us with certain types of problems but not others. It is important to discern who is best for what in your circle of family, friends, and acquaintances.

Jean, for example, has a friend who is very pessimistic and anxious about anything to do with children. One day Jean mistakenly went to her friend Alice for reassurance about her oldest child, who had a high fever and strep throat. But Alice dwelled on the pessimistic side of Jean's problem and even gave Jean doubts about her child's ability to recover. Instead of getting the comfort, support, and reassurance that she needed, Jean just became more anxious and more tense than ever. She had acted impulsively against her own interests when she confided in Alice. If she had taken a few minutes to think about it, Jean would have realized that Alice couldn't give her what she needed at that time and that she would more likely be dragged down by talking to Alice about children. What would have helped Jean would have been to talk to her friend Ann, who had been through many of her own children's illnesses and could have warmly and genuinely reassured Jean. But in her anxiety, Jean didn't take the time to think through her choice.

When you reach out to someone to help you take care of your needs, pause and think a few minutes about whom to approach. Who can best help you get what you want and need? Try talking to that person. See how you feel afterward. Do you feel satisfied and fulfilled, or are you left feeling frustrated and ill at ease? Then decide whether that person was appropriate for that situation.

It might be helpful to keep a list of your friends, relatives, and colleagues, noting their strengths and weaknesses as confidants. Then when you want to speak to someone about something important, you can review your list and choose the best person for that particular problem. Leave space on your list to keep track of each time you confide in them, the nature of your discussion, and the emotional outcome, that is, the degree of satisfaction that you feel as a result of talk. Did the discussion satisfy your particular needs? Your feeling afterward will be the best indicator of how appropriate your choice of person was. Also, check and see how you are feeling a few hours later. Did you get a momentary rush of relief but then feel wanting again? Or did the contact have a lasting effect? In other words, did you learn something from the contact that changed your outlook, or did you get some tender loving care that helped carry you through for a time? Both are valuable; yet it is important to know which you can receive from whom.

This week think about whom you trust. This new awareness will help you refine your understanding of your relationships and enable you to get what you need more easily. One word of warning: Be aware of your friends' and acquaintances' strengths and limitations without being judgmental. See them for who they are in all their humanness, and appreciate each of them for what they can give.

Exaggerations are stressful.

Sally has a tendency to speak in extremes. She is very dramatic and therefore seems very alive to those around her. When she tells you a story, it's always the *best* thing that ever happened to her, the *most beautiful* sunset she's ever seen, or the *worst* thing someone could have done to her. Yet Sally is neither very satisfied in her life nor very effective. She is living on an emotional roller coaster: either full of high hopes for life always going just her way simply because something positive has happened to her or bereft because things are not going her way and never will.

Of course, neither one of Sally's conclusions could possibly be true: Life is never either all good or all bad but rather a mixture of both. Sally does not recognize shades of gray or realize that things usually change. To her, everything is black or white.

In reality, life is full of shades of gray. Many things appear clouded at first, only later to be seen for what they truly are. There are many areas in which we have to compromise. Situations that are less than ideal eventually can become satisfactory.

Staying clear of extremes can help prevent the emotional roller coaster that Sally and many of us ride on.

Seeing in extremes is often an attempt to feel more excited (and therefore more alive) or an attempt to simplify something that is complicated. The cost of this pseudoexcitement and simplification is stress, emotional imbalance, and a loss of clarity.

Thinking in extremes is stressful because you begin to believe the exaggerated evaluations of situations and react to them emotionally as if they were reality. For example, if your financial situation is tight, you can acknowledge that and think about why and how it can be changed. Or you can think about all the dreadful things that could make it worse: You could lose your job; you could lose your home; you could go cold and hungry; your bank could close.

Obviously, one reaction to the first evaluation would be to take control, finding practical ways to improve it. A typical response to the extreme picture would be to feel overwhelmed and despondent, thereby undermining any attempts to change it.

You will find that you have typical patterns and places where you use extremes for specific reasons. Perhaps you may find that you exaggerate in the positive direction in order to impress your boss or that you may exaggerate in the negative direction with your friends to elicit sympathy and special treatment.

Neither situation works to your advantage. Your boss will expect the extremely positive outcomes you have boasted about and require an explanation about why you haven't produced them, and your friends will soon become skeptical of your need for sympathy when they realize that things are not really as bad as you said. Now you will have to deal not only with their reactions but also with the part of you that feels a bit guilty for being manipulative through exaggeration.

This week we are going to become conscious of whether and how much we exaggerate and make an attempt to balance it. For the first three days this week, pay attention to when you speak in unnecessary extremes. Make note of the situations that lead you to exaggerate. Try to pinpoint a pattern for your actions. See how you feel when you speak in extremes. Does it give you an exaggerated sense of euphoria or despair? Are you stressing yourself by using extremes?

For each of the last four days, choose one situation in which you commonly use extremes and decide to speak in a more balanced, accurate way. Make an attempt to catch yourself before you speak. If you hear yourself exaggerating, catch yourself and change your communication. It may be something as simple as responding to a simple "How are you today?" You might say, "Terrible" or "Wonderful" when "I'm okay" and "Good" might be even more accurate.

Remember, what you say affects you. It is important to be honest to yourself about whatever is happening. Avoid extremes this week and reduce your stress level.

I build a loving support system.

"No man is an island. No man stands alone." We all recognize these familiar lines. The words are true. Human beings are social animals who don't do well standing alone. Newborns kept socially isolated fail to thrive. The severest punishment used in prisons is isolation. And yet many of us, even though we may not be isolated in the strictest sense, do suffer isolation from a loving support system.

A support system means people with whom we truly can be ourselves. People who accept us as we are; who will not judge but love us at our worst; who help us feel good when we are down; who will risk telling us the truth about their feelings and hear the truth of ours; who are there when we need them and will come to us in need; and who will listen to us and help us unravel our problems. In short, a group of good friends.

Without a network of loving friends we endure a kind of isolation; an alienation from our true selves and the true selves of others. Lacking this, we suffer from the stress of trying to do it all by ourselves. This is unnecessary and depleting.

The importance of having people on our side cannot be

overestimated. Yet the intimacy involved is difficult for many people. Many of us fear that self-revelation will lead to rejection. We judge ourselves and fear that others will, too. We may fear that the information we reveal will be used against us. We may fear that others will take advantage of our apparent "weakness' when we are in need. While these are all possibilities, if we develop our friendships with care and common sense, we will minimize the chance of betrayal.

Friendship grows slowly with experience and trust. We need to choose friends with whom we feel comfortable and open. Friends with whom we can laugh and have fun. Friends who understand and respect us. Friends with whom we share interests and viewpoints. Friends who will share themselves with us and with whom we want to share ourselves.

This week take stock of your support system. Are your friends truly supportive? Can you trust them? Do you enjoy your time with them? Do you feel better about yourself after having been with them?

For the first day think about your friends and ask the questions above. Are you in relationships in which you are not comfortable, and yet you continue with them? Are there relationships you really enjoy and yet in which you do not invest your time? Do you have the kind of friendships that are supportive, or do you need to develop them?

On the second day make a list of your friends and what you want to do to increase the supportiveness of your relationships. Map out a plan. There may be areas of conflict to be resolved with some people. There may be needs you have not expressed to others. There may be areas of irritation you have to heal. There may be expressions of affection you need to reveal. There may be doubts you want to discuss. Plan to mend any areas in the relationships which keep you and your friend from being more open with each other.

On the third to seventh days, choose one or more of these friendships and begin to build more closeness. Take small steps if you need to. This takes courage and humility. How does it feel to reveal more of yourself? Do you feel closer, more trusting? Do you feel more supported? Reveal your needs in the relationship to the other person. Can the two of you come to an understanding about what each wants and the other can give? Can you understand each other's sensitive points, respect and accept them?

You may discover you want to find some new friends. That, of course, is not always easy. Yet you can keep yourself in tune with your desires and be aware when you are with someone with whom you feel especially good. You can then try to foster a friendship with that person.

In either case, be sensitive and go slowly. Let the movement come naturally from within and don't force it. Be honest with your feelings and build your support system gradually.

Take stock of your support system this week. You'll feel better about yourself.

I can alleviate my guilt.

☐

Guilt may be as comfortable as your favorite pair of slippers, but those slippers might as well be cement blocks. Guilt is tremendously undermining and draining when it is not serving its true purpose: to alert us when we err.

Holding on to inappropriate guilt has many stressful consequences. It diminishes self-esteem and feelings of worthiness. It reduces positive assertiveness and a sense of one's own authority. It elicits self-punishment, such as self-destructive behavior, failure, and inability to enjoy pleasure. It leads one to expect less of oneself than is possible. And it reduces available energy.

The problem with guilt is that for many of us it was used as a way to control our behavior when we were children, and it continues to evoke the same reactions in us as adults. The difference, of course, is that as adults we are in charge of our lives. But when we feel guilty, we often begin to feel like children.

This week we will begin to learn to alleviate guilt by differentiating between real and false guilt. Real guilt is a result of intentional dishonesty, ignoring of responsibilities, and disregarding personal contracts. It is a feeling that indicates that we have erred and need to reconsider our course of action. It requires corrective measures that will eliminate or greatly reduce the guilt.

It is easy to illustrate real guilt. Most of us feel it when we lie, steal, or take unfair advantage of someone. It is the feeling we have when we know we have done something wrong.

False guilt, on the other hand, is primarily in one's mind. The outer situation does not truly merit guilt, and yet we feel guilty because we misunderstand the situation. False guilt can result from believing what someone else tells you only because of your relationship to that person. It may come from an exaggerated sense of your responsibilities. It may result from leftover childhood feelings.

An example of false guilt is feeling guilty when we fail to complete an overwhelming amount of tasks. Our error was in thinking that it was possible to complete them, or perhaps in not asking for help with them. There is no basis for real guilt here. Our intent was positive: to take care of the responsibilities. The fact that they were not completed was a result of our miscalculation, not our bad character. character.

The exercise this week will help you separate your feelings of real and false guilt and then alleviate the guilt feelings through forgiveness and action.

Do this exercise throughout the week. Begin by observing what makes you feel guilty. Decide whether it is real or false guilt. Whichever it is, forgive yourself.

Then for one instance of real guilt, take corrective action. Either speak to the person involved and clarify and change the situation, or do what you need to correct the situation and make it truthful. If it is an ongoing habit, such as being late and keeping people waiting, be on time this week. If it is a lie you told, tell the truth and face the consequences.

The benefits of relieving guilt are tremendous. You will find yourself feeling lighter and freer. You will find flow where you previously found obstruction. You will have more self-respect and be able to accept more pleasure and fulfillment in your life. Unburden yourself. Drop some guilt this week.

I feel as well as I eat.

One of the ways we stress ourselves is by eating unhealthy foods. Our bodies are electrochemical machines. What we put into them directly affects how they function. We wouldn't consider putting diesel fuel into a gasoline-powered engine, and yet we are often quite unconscious about how we fuel our own engines, our bodies.

Foods either can provide healthy nourishment for our bodies or can stress them. To make it easiest for our bodies to stay healthy, it is important to know the difference and to avoid too many high-stress foods.

How can foods stress the body? One way is by providing empty calories. White sugar and alcohol are high-stress foods: They provide nothing nutritional to the body except calories. They make the body work to digest and remove them from the system. And they often contribute to excess weight, which stresses all the body systems.

Caffeine is another high-stress item. Caffeine artificially stimulates the body, putting it unnecessarily on alert. The nervous system is stimulated and stays that way until the effect wears off and we feel let down. The body also works to remove the caffeine. It may feel good to get that energy boost, but the cost is high.

Eating junk foods is another way of stressing the body with food. They provide empty calories, can make us overweight, add excess salt (which can raise blood pressure), contain preservatives (which have been correlated with diseases), and may, by filling us up, prevent us from eating something more nutritious.

Refined white flour and its products deplete the body of vitamins, causing stress.

There are foods that cause subtle food allergies, acting like small amounts of poison to the body. Two common ones are wheat and dairy products. They can cause symptoms such as headaches, fuzzy-headedness, indigestion, diarrhea, and lack of energy.

This week's exercises will be about watching what you eat and changing how you eat.

For the first three days, simply observe what and how you eat and how you feel. Do you eat regular meals? Do you eat high-stress foods? Do you eat a balanced diet (some food from each food group: grain; dairy; fruits and vegetables; meat, chicken, fish, or other high-protein foods)? How do you feel? Do you have lots of energy? Are you clearheaded? Are you free from aches and pains? Are you emotionally even, or are you on a roller coaster, with lots of highs and lows?

For the last four days, change how you eat. Eat in a less stressful way. Lower your intake of one or more high-stress foods. Eliminate some if you want. Do you crave what you have limited or eliminated? See if you notice any difference in how you feel both emotionally and physically. Do you have more or less energy?

The point of this exercise is to raise your awareness of what and how you eat and how it affects you. Then you will have more information on which to base your choices about your regular eating habits.

Changing your eating habits is best approached gingerly, for many emotions are attached to food. It is important to accept yourself and your particular food habits, as they are probably deeply ingrained. Be gentle with yourself, checking to make sure that you are not setting yourself up for failure by making the task too difficult. If you are under a lot of stress, make only small changes now and wait for a more relaxed time to make others. If you revert to foods that you decided not to eat, acknowledge that and simply commit yourself *again* to not eating them. Forgive yourself for stumbling, pick yourself up, and start again.

Remember, the goal for this week is simply to raise your consciousness about what you eat so that you can be more aware in your choices. Bon appétit!

I don't procrastinate: I do it now.

Each one of us knows the part of us that would rather put off until tomorrow what we can do today. Some of us do this more than others. The unfortunate result of such behavior is that we clutter our lives with chores and errands left undone. In addition, we clutter our minds trying to remember to do them! All this clutter is stressful.

The simplest thing to do, if possible, is to take care of things when you think of them. For example, if you notice that you have to empty the wastebasket, why wait? Do it and get it over with. If you know you have to remember to take something with you tomorrow, put it in your bag or briefcase right now. If you have to defrost something from the freezer, take it out now.

This week pay attention to your pattern of dealing with chores and tasks and begin to develop the habit of taking care of them promptly.

For the first three days, observe how you deal with tasks and chores. Do you notice them and ignore them? Do you notice them, acknowledge them, and put them off until later? Do you notice them and deal with them immediately? Do your chores usually get done, or are they often left undone? Do you feel free from chores or burdened by them?

For the next four days, take care of whatever chores can be done as you notice them. If they can't be handled efficiently at that moment, start a list, and keep track of what has to be done. Allow some time each day to deal with the chores on the list.

By your dealing with things as they occur, the list should not become burdensome. The tasks will be accomplished and you will feel up-to-date and relieved of carrying them with you.

Avoid procrastinating this week. Do it now and let go of some stress.

I allow some time to play.

We are all children at heart. We all need a good bout of playing regularly, or we lose touch with the child in us. Playing is a wonderful way of relieving stress and nurturing ourselves. It is a time when we can lose control, be silly, stop feeling responsible, make mistakes that don't matter, and have a rollicking good time. Playing relieves pressure, gives us a feeling of freedom, and leaves us refreshed and ready to face the world.

Surprisingly enough, many of us have resistance to playing. When we do have the free time to play, it is interesting how few of us use it that way. More adult, constructive, and responsible activities often take precedence. Other less-active pastimes such as watching TV, listening to music, and visiting with friends are easier and often supplant playtime. Not to belittle these activities, but they are very different from what is meant by play.

Playing is silly, funny, and engrossing. It is a frolic. It can take many forms, from something as unstructured as a pillow fight to as organized a game as Monopoly. Whatever shape it takes, it is a way to divert the adult and call forth the child.

Many of us dismiss playing as unimportant, beneath us,

or as a waste of time. What most of us are really saying is that it is something we are supposed to leave behind with our childhood. Playing is for kids.

Many of us truly are out of the habit and ignore our need for it. We have developed an image of what being an adult means, and it is not often in that image. The truth is that as adults we like the position of being in control, and playing often means losing control. We may also feel silly, foolish, or inadequate when we play.

It is not always easy to overcome these feelings and want to engage in play, and yet the payoff for doing so is great. If you have children, it's a great way of strengthening your bonds and deepening your relationships with them. And whether you have children or not, playing helps you deepen your relationship with your own inner child. In so doing, you tap a source of creativity and energy that we often ignore.

This week use the first two days to examine your attitudes toward play. Observe how you feel around playful people or what you do if someone approaches you playfully. Do you welcome him or reject him? Do you like it and reach for more, or do you disapprove and push it away? When you see kids playing, do you usually want to control the play, or do you wistfully remember what is was like to be a kid?

For the next two days, think of ways in which you want to play. You might like card or board games, sports, word games, contact games like pillow fights or wrestling, sex play, acting, water play, mental play, imaginary voyages, painting and drawing, using clay, or whatever gives you a sense of freedom and play. Make a list of twenty ways you like to play.

For the last three days, spend at least a total of three hours playing. It could be an hour each day or three hours in one day. Use the time to play, be silly, laugh, feel free and childlike. See how it feels. It may take a little getting used to at first. You might be rusty, but persevere, and see how you like it. It usually feels wonderful.

One word of warning. Do not take your play too seriously or use it to put demands on yourself to do better and better. This is a time to just be yourself as you are.

Allow some time to play this week. You'll love yourself for it!

I can accept criticism with dignity.

Criticism can elicit many feelings. We are often caught in the bind of either denying the validity of the criticism we receive or accepting it and feeling we are bad. It is possible to understand that we can be in the wrong and not feel as if we should be punished. It is the value judgment that *wrong* is the equivalent of *bad* that prevents us from wanting to admit when we are wrong.

We pay a high price for always trying to be right. Trying to uphold an unrealistic image of ourselves as perfect can be exhausting. We are always a bit on edge, trying not to err and denying our mistakes. We spend precious energy trying to avoid the feelings that can emerge when we sense we are wrong: shame, embarrassment, fear, self-hate. Although we'd prefer to avoid examining these emotions, they serve as good indicators of where to look to make change.

When we have uncomfortable feelings such as shame or embarrassment, it is a signal to step back a bit and examine the situation. Shame or embarrassment could be a clue that we truly deserve the criticism. At other times the same feelings may simply be a result of old patterns of response and not warranted by the situation. By making this deter-

69

mination, we can decide whether or not the criticism has merit.

If the criticism is reasonable, we can accept it with dignity and take appropriate action. If it is not, we can explain why we disagree.

This week we are going to learn how to deal with criticism.

For the first three days, observe yourself when you are criticized. How do you react to being told you did something wrong? Do you get defensive and reel off a list of how that couldn't be so? Do you feel so bad about yourself that you collapse and become unable to mobilize yourself to do anything? Do you feel hurt and angry and argue with the other person? Do you accept being criticized with dignity? Do you carefully examine the content of what the other person says, accepting the truth and pointing out the errors?

What kind of feelings do you have during this kind of interaction? Are you anxious? Scared? Arrogant? Angry? At peace? Compassionate? Concerned? Interested? Willing to participate?

On the fourth day, think about how you could have handled these situations by assuming responsibility without feeling that you were bad. Try to remove yourself from the situation and see it from the outside as an impartial observer would. (Admittedly, this is difficult, but it can be very rewarding.) Be honest about your part in the situation. Could you have done anything to prevent it? What would the impartial observer say to you? To the other person? What can you do to resolve the conflict? Acknowledging one's errors can be humbling, but it also relieves you and builds self-respect.

On the fifth, sixth, and seventh days, learn to react in a new way to three similar situations in which you are criticized. Try to consider and accept the criticism. It may be necessary to slow down your interaction and step back from it emotionally in order to be able to handle it. See clearly and acknowledge what you may have contributed to creating the situation. If possible, try to change the situation.

Throughout the week, be aware of how you feel about being criticized. Make sure you do not blame or punish yourself. Accept your limitations and give yourself credit for the acts of courage you are performing. Allow your self-esteem to grow as your dignity expands.

Accept criticism with dignity this week. You'll grow from it!

Sex can increase or decrease stress.

The idealized view of sex—two people falling into each other's arms, passionately embracing, pleasuring each other until they come together in the ecstasy of mutual orgasm—is hardly the usual human sexual encounter. To you for whom this is commonplace, congratulations! For the rest of us, we need to examine our relationship to our sexuality to find out whether we allow sex to increase or to decrease stress.

Sex can be stressful if we burden ourselves with self-evaluations based on our sexual experiences. For example, a person lacking sexual desire can feel inadequate and guilty for his or her inability to perform sexually. This complicates the issue of lack of desire, so that the person is dealing not only with a sexual issue but now also with an issue of self-worth.

But if it can be kept simply a sexual issue, you can probably resolve it more easily. This is most likely with a supportive and understanding mate, one who can help you go through the process of resolving the problem rather than one who is feeling threatened, angry, and therefore blames you.

By removing the pointed finger of blame, and the resulting guilt, a burden has been lifted, a stress removed.

On the brighter side, satisfying sex can relieve tension tremendously. It is nature's best tranquilizer. A good orgasm releases built-up tensions. This essential activity, however, is not always given the priority it deserves in our lives. Many obstacles keep us from frequently having good sex. We are influenced by our negative attitudes toward sex, the pace of our lives, easier alternatives, such as TV, and interpersonal disharmonies. It is not uncommon for a couple who have some alone time in the evening to complain of either being too tired for sex or watching TV and avoiding each other.

Sex is equally important for those of us without partners. We are still sexual beings with sexual appetites and needs. We have the option of masturbation, and it is an important one. If you do not currently have a sexual partner and you do not masturbate, consider seriously your attitudes toward masturbation, with an intent toward changing them.

This week decide which group you fall into: a person whose tension is increased by your relationship to sexuality, or someone whose tension is decreased by sexuality. (You may fall into a different group at different times. Decide which group you fall into this week.)

For those of you in the first group, whose tension is increased by sexuality, use an affirmation to accept your sexual limitation. Say or write the following as often as you feel comfortable every day for seven days: "I am a lovable, loving human being with sexual feelings."

To those of you in the second group, who have satisfying sex that decreases tension: Ask yourself if you make sex as high a priority as it deserves. Do you really want to see that TV show, or would you really benefit more from the closeness and release of some good sex? If you theoretically would prefer more sex and don't know why you are not arranging your life to accommodate it, ask yourself why and how you could manage it.

This week make sex a priority and observe why it loses importance for you if it does. Then you will have some information that will enable you to make a more conscious choice.

Sex can certainly become a complex concern. Yet we can, with some attention, make it a gratifying release that reduces tension. It is unnecessary to burden ourselves with self-judgements when we meet our sexual limitations. And it's important to make it a priority when it's satisfying. Let sex be fun. You'll enjoy it!

Physical fitness makes me feel good.

Would you buy an inexpensive product that guaranteed to do the following: increase your vitality; improve your sex life; make you sleep better; increase your feelings of self-esteem; decrease your weight; improve your appearance; eliminate constipation; remove waste products from your body; relax you; decrease the aging process; increase your cardiopulmonary efficiency; improve your circulation; give you an overall sense of well-being?

Of course you would! It seems almost too good to be true. What could do all that?

Exercise!

The body was meant to move. Lack of exercise is stressful to it. The body functions and feels best when it is moved regularly and pushed to its limits. Flexibility, muscle tone, and strength increase and circulation improves. Waste removal is enhanced by increased respirations, circulation, and sweating. Heart and lung capacity increase. Excess calories are burned rather than turned into fat. Endorphins, chemicals released in the brain after sufficient exercise, contribute to feelings of well-being and relaxation, helping to improve sleep and sex. The aging process is slowed by the improved circulation and decreased body weight.

Lack of exercise stresses the body by not facilitating all these processes.

You can have your daily exercise needs met in such a variety of ways that you should never get bored. Easiest is to find a home exercise program. There are books, audio- and videotapes, and records to help with this. The advantages to home exercise are that it is inexpensive, always available, and requires no traveling.

In addition to this, you can swim, jog, play competitive sports (tennis, raquetball, handball, volleyball, basketball, softball, golf, bowling), go to a gym for workouts and classes, have an exercise instructor come to your home, or do it along with a TV program. Any kind of exercise is fine, as long as it includes time for flexibility, strengthening, and cardiovascular fitness. (This last requirement is often satisfied by aerobic workouts.)

A word of caution: Although exercise is good for and necessary for everybody, some people must be very careful about what kind and how much exercise they do. If you know you have had cardiac or circulatory difficulties, it is essential that you check with your physician for exercise guidelines. If you cannot easily walk two miles, or if you have chest pain, light-headedness, fainting, stomach or bowel upset, flu-type symptoms, or respiratory difficulties after mild exercise, see your doctor immediately, certainly before you begin an exercise program.

Your assignment this week is to make a commitment to exercising in some way at least ten minutes a day each day. More time is better if you can. Start gently and do not force yourself beyond what is reasonably comfortable. (Don't create pain as an excuse for not exercising, and don't make yourself exercise if it's really painful.)

If you can extend this commitment into and through next week, you will really be on your way to making daily exercise a way of life. Two weeks is a good foundation for a new habit—feeling the benefits by then will encourage you to continue.

Find some exercise that is fun to do and help yourself become physically fit. Enjoy yourself!

I drop an unhealthy habit.

You wouldn't think of doing housework with a weight strapped on your back, would you? Housework is something we try to do as quickly and easily as possible. And yet we handicap our bodies almost as much by indulging in unhealthy habits. The stress these bad habits create takes energy that could be used for something positive and pleasurable.

Most of us have one or more of these deleterious habits. Which is yours? Cigarettes? Drugs (recreational, over-the-counter & prescription)? Caffeine? Sugar? Alcohol? Faulty hygiene (skin, teeth, hair)? Poor elimination? Erratic sleep patterns? Inadequate exercise? Unhealthy eating habits?

The stress created by ingesting unhealthy substances is analagous to self-poisoning: The body is fed toxic substances that it must clear away. The digestive, the excretory, and the circulatory systems must work harder to eliminate them. Each substance affects the nervous system in an unnatural way, stressing it. Cigarettes give conflicting messages, both to relax and speed up (simultaneously depleting vitamin C). Each drug has a myriad of individual harmful effects. Caffeine speeds everything up. Sugar gives a sudden energy rush followed by a rapid marked letdown. Alcohol is a depressant. Each one works the body a little harder than necessary for no healthy benefit.

Self-care habits are also important in limiting stress. Maintaining our bodies by keeping them clean inside and out, feeding them, exercising them, and resting them is important to keep them functioning properly.

The assignment this week is to choose just one habit and either decrease or eliminate it.

Observe how you react to the idea of decreasing this habit. This habit has served a purpose in your life, and at some level, you probably won't want to give it up. This is your resistance. It may not be obvious immediately, but be watchful for it. This is what prevents you from eliminating bad habits. Respect this resistance. Accept that it is there, and then make a choice to not indulge in that habit this week despite your resistance.

Pay attention to your emotional reactions this week when you resist the habit or when you take better care of yourself. Write down any persistent emotions or feelings. At the end of the week, notice how you feel about yourself, having decreased or given up this habit. In order to establish this in your daily life, continue for one more week and then decide whether to keep it.

Now don't get the impression here that the aim is to be a puritan. What is important is to identify which habits you have that are most interfering with harmonious functioning in your life, and deal with them. But be gentle with yourself. You are not a bad person just because you have a bad habit, and you are not a weak person just because you can't overcome it. It takes patience, humility, acceptance, and determination to change our unhealthy habits. Start over again when you falter. Be understanding and forgiving with yourself. This week change your unhealthy habit with gentleness.

I let my anger go.

Anger is a potent emotion that is natural and protective. It arises in us when we feel threatened or hurt and serves to trigger the fight or flight mechanism so that we can fight back. Too often, however, anger is triggered when our feelings are hurt rather than when we are in real danger. This causes us to react with the same intensity as if we were in mortal danger.

For that reason, anger can become a problematic emotion. Intense anger may lead to hostility and physical violence. Anger may be expressed as cynicism and sarcasm, which interferes with harmonious relationships. It can undermine good performance and wreck marriages. Needless to say, anger is the cause of much stress in our lives.

One of the other big problems with anger is that we are afraid to show it. We fear losing the other person's approval if we show our anger; because of that, we avoid expressing it directly. Often people unwilling to express their anger may become sullen and withdrawn, even depressed.

If we could let go of the need for the other's approval, and have the courage to express our anger calmly and directly, we could avoid many such misunderstandings.

This week try to recognize your anger and express it calmly and directly. For the first three days, observe yourself, and discover what and who triggers your anger.

Keep notes on a small notepad and notice what makes you angry and who you allow to anger you. What kind of conditions make you mad? Frustration, fear, discomfort, pain, hurt pride, or criticism? What kind of attitudes trigger strong reactions in you: condescension, whining, arrogance, nonchalance, placating, authoritarianism, self-effacement? Which people often make you angry? How do you deal with your anger? Does your pulse race and your temper boil? Or are you the cool type, who goes into a deep freeze when angry? Do you withdraw and hold on to your anger? Do you deny your anger, pretending it does not exist? Do you scream and try to scare others? And to whom is it most difficult to show your anger?

For the last four days, practice showing your anger effectively. For those of us who are explosive when angry, this means containing our anger, and for those of us who withhold our anger, it means expressing it. If you are an explosive type, try to step back from the anger. A few ways of doing this are: counting to ten; imagining the person standing before you in his or her underwear; thinking of all the things you like about the other person; taking four or more deep breaths; walking around to settle yourself before talking; and postponing the confrontation until you have your emotions under better control.

When you finally feel ready to confront the other person calmly, speak in as gentle a tone and language as you can and keep breathing deeply. It probably will feel good to assert some control over the anger.

If you withhold your anger, choose one or more instances in which you would rather avoid the other person. Summon enough courage to confront him or her in a calm, clear manner. Be prepared to stay calm even if you meet frustration and resistance. No one likes to acknowledge that he or she has made someone else angry, and often the other person will become defensive, denying his or her responsibility. The object here is simply to express ourselves, not to convince the other person of our position.

How did it feel to take that step? You will probably be a bit anxious or frightened at first, but this feeling will decrease as you become more practiced. Eventually your anger will lessen and your self-respect will grow. When you start to feel better about yourself, anger (yours and others') will have less and less of an effect on you.

If you can't bring youself to confront someone with your anger, or if you are in a situation in which you truly can't confront someone with your anger, write your anger out on paper. Spell out all your complaints and problems and vent all your venom. Let yourself go. Then, when you've completely depleted your anger, rip the paper into lots of little pieces and throw it away.

The most important thing to remember this week is that our anger hurts us more than it hurts others. We do ourselves a favor when we release it.

Take care of yourself this week. Let some anger go.

I need deep relaxation.

After spending days pursuing our goals and tending to our tasks, we each need time to take a minivacation from the world. Deep relaxation can be such a vacation. It is a time when cares and worries are left behind and we are surrounded with relaxing thoughts and feelings. The focus is on your muscles, but the relaxing feelings will take you over, leaving you refreshed and enlivened.

You will find that some days are more difficult than others and will leave you more stressed. Choose one of the tough days this week and spend twenty minutes to one half hour immersing yourself in this deep relaxation exercise.

Find a quiet spot where you will not be interrupted. Turn off the telephone. Put up a Do Not Disturb sign. And do whatever else you think is necessary to ensure that you will be left alone.

Turn off the lights. Lie down and make yourself as comfortable as possible. Change your position and vary the arrangement of pillows to make sure you are as relaxed as you can be. Check and be certain that all your body parts are supported and that your muscles aren't working unnecessarily.

Now sense into your feet by paying attention to the feeling in them. Is there any tension there? Imagine the tension melting and running down and out your toes. Picture it flowing out like a river. Now feel into your ankles. Are they at all tense? Breathe into the tension and let it go so that it flows through your feet and out your toes.

Now your calves. Check for any tension there. Breathe into it and let it flow down and out through your feet and toes. Move up into your knees. Explore your knees, looking for tension. Again allow the tension to melt and flow down the calves, through the ankles and feet, and out the toes. Next your thighs. Thighs very often have deep tension, so spend some time sensing deeply into your thighs, allowing any tension to come into your consciousness. When you sense it, breathe into it and let it melt, slowly flowing down the legs, to the knees, through the calves, to the ankles, into the feet, and out the toes.

Now check the entire length of both of your legs. Are they still relaxed? Has any tension surfaced that you didn't notice before? If so, allow that tension to melt and flow down and out. Both of your legs should be very relaxed by now. Feel how heavy they seem, and how good it feels not to have to do any work to hold them up. Feel the support underneath them and be grateful to that support for holding up your legs.

Now move up to the pelvic area. Check the area of your genitals, pelvis, and your lower abdomen. Is there tension here? Breathe into any tension and allow it to melt, flowing down and out your legs and feet. Feel the relaxation come as the tension melts. Check your lower back. Breathe into any tension there. Feel it melting and flowing down and out your legs and toes. Move up into your upper abdomen and your midback. Sense into them for any tension. Feel how good it feels to breathe into it, melting it and letting it relax and flow down and out your legs and feet.

You are feeling more and more relaxed now. Your body is feeling very, very heavy, and it feels very good. Now sense into your chest and your upper back. Through your breathing, melt any tension there. Breathe deeply into any areas where some tension might remain and let the tension melt and flow down and out of your body. Now move into your shoulders, arms, and hands. Check them slowly and carefully, as much tension is often held here. Breathe slowly and deeply into your shoulders, arms, and hands, releasing the tension as you go, so that it can flow out and down the body, exiting from the toes.

Now sense into the neck and the head. Feel into the forehead, the ears, the mouth, the jaw, the eyes, the nose, the scalp. Let go any tension in each of those areas. Breathe it down and out the body, feeling it ride on your breath as it flows away.

Now your entire body is relaxed. Feel what a relief it is not to have to hold it up. Feel gravity pulling you into its support.

Use this time to let your imagination run wild. Go to your favorite place (the ocean, the mountains, a favorite garden, a shopping mall, a restaurant). Explore a place you've never visited (another country, another planet). Spend some time with someone you love or admire, perhaps even someone who has already died or has yet to be born. Do something crazy or impossible. Invent something. See colors that don't exist. In short, have fun with your imagination. Use this time to do something that makes you feel happy and fulfilled. Remember, this is your minivacation from the real world. It is entirely yours. Make it whatever you want it to be.

This exercise is best done either by thoroughly familiarizing yourself with the concept and the sequence or by making a tape recording of it in a very soft, gently coaxing voice. Choose the way that makes it easiest for you to relax. Make sure that you spend enough time with each body part so that you feel fully relaxed in that part before you move on.

When you have finished the exercise, gently bring yourself back to the world by slowly moving your feet and hands, your legs and arms, sitting up slowly, rubbing your arms, legs, trunk, and face, opening your eyes and looking around. You surely will feel very different from when you began.

Bon voyage!

I order my time with a schedule.

☐

Time is a concept that enables us to organize our lives. Time that is in disorder is stressful, because not everything gets done and we feel hassled.

Tim faced this dilemma of time in disorder. He was trying to manage his job, his family life, and go to school. He had many responsibilities, all demanding his time and attention. He was struggling. Finally he came to realize that he could lessen his struggle by organizing his time.

Tim guessed correctly that he was using his time inefficiently. When he took the time, precious as it seemed, to sit down and organize his week, he found that indeed he could attend to all his tasks and still have some time left over. Tim felt good when he had done this and even better when he knew that by his keeping to his schedule, everything would get done, and he would still have free time.

Time management is a skill that you can develop with a little time and attention. But first you must convince yourself that you want and need to do it. So for the first three days this week, observe yourself move through your day. Is there time left over in which you feel free, or are you doing something every minute? Do you squander time because you don't have something to do when you have a few extra minutes? Do you find yourself spending extended periods of time chatting with friends or daydreaming when you need to be attending to chores? Do you get involved unnecessarily with details when you could get more done as well without them? Are you thrown by the unexpected to the point where you don't know to get back on track?

By the end of the three days, you will have a sense of how you handle your time. On the fourth day, plan your time schedule. Sit down and list all the things you have to do every day. Then make a list of the things you have to do weekly and monthly.

Now, with this information, organize your day around your daily activities, allotting the time you think they will require, plus 10 percent for underestimation and the unexpected. Do this for each day until your week is complete.

At this point, find places in your daily schedules to include the weekly and monthly tasks, allowing about 10 percent more time than you expect for each task. Leave some open spaces in each day for the unexpected.

Things to remember to include in your schedule are: personal needs (eating, sleeping, exercising, social, play, sex, maintenance); vocational (job duties, phone calls, vocational education, networking); financial (bookkeeping, bill paying, banking, education, consulting with professionals); social (phone calls, meetings, parties, dinners, sports); family (phone calls, time together, hugging, discussions, family decision-making and planning); and spiritual (church, praying, meditating, visualizing).

For the last three days of the week, use this new schedule. Does it work for you? Make the adjustments necessary so that it is realistic for your needs. At first you may need to make many adjustments as you use it. Later there will be fewer changes, as you become more accurate in your estimations.

Use this schedule as a guideline, open to constant revision. Work with the schedule, constantly updating it as your needs change. See it as a servant rather than a master. Happy scheduling!

I keep an open mind.

Keeping an open mind is one way to limit stress. When our minds are open, our options are open. When our minds are open, our energies flow. When our minds are open, we can feel optimistic.

A closed mind, on the other hand, can create stress. A closed mind limits our options, and thereby causes us to feel trapped and impotent. A closed mind can waste energy and cause unnecessary conflict with others.

It is important to keep an open mind, because even if we are sure we are right, there is always the possibility we could be wrong. Equally important is that it feels better to keep our minds open.

For example, Jane had bought a microwave oven to put over the stove in her very small kitchen. When she went to have it installed, she discovered that it would be unsafe to mount it above her stove. This upset her, as she had no other wall space, and the only other possibility would be to put it on her counter.

Jane was sure that she would never be able to function in a kitchen with less counter space than she already had. She was so upset just thinking about it that she was ready to take the microwave right back to the store. Her husband, Jim, however, wanted the microwave.

Jane was a mess. She got irritable, felt trapped, and felt deprived. She finally had to leave the house to cool off. When she returned, Jim had installed the microwave on the counter. Jane had decidedly mixed feelings about it.

After a week of using the microwave, however, Jane did acknowledge that the convenience afforded her more than outweighed the loss of counter space, which she hardly noticed.

Had Jane kept an open mind initially, she would have saved herself the exhausting upset, the loss of time and energy, and the conflict with Jim. It would have been much easier for her to have said, "Okay. I'll try it on the counter and then decide."

This week for the first three days, pay attention to whether you close your mind by taking a rigid stance. It may be in a simple discussion, or it may be in making a decision. Observe yourself and notice especially how you feel when you do it. Do you feel tight and tense or loose and relaxed?

For the last four days, attempt to soften your stance and open your mind at least once each day. When you find yourself gearing up to take a rigid stance, take a few deep breaths, ask yourself how important it is that you be right, or that you maintain your position, then let down and open your mind to other possibilities.

It is not important that in the end you may return to your original position. What is important is that you go through the process of opening yourself to other possibilities.

Give yourself a break this week. Open your mind.

I face an anxiety.

We're all familiar with the experience of avoiding situations that cause us anxiety. We can think of excuse after excuse about why it doesn't have to be done now, why it would be better to wait, why we have other things to do that are more important. And we allow ourselves to put off dealing with these anxiety-laden situations. The result of this procrastination is that we have them, as well as the anxiety they create, hanging over us.

Stress certainly is caused by not dealing with situations that produce anxiety. We all know what they are: going to the doctor or dentist; doing our taxes; writing our will; making hospital visits to our sick friends and relatives; confronting someone with something unpleasant; finishing assignments; or anything that you have to do and don't want to.

We torture ourselves by not dealing with these things and getting them over with. We deny them and try to forget they exist or talk ourselves out of them by rationalizing, but we know the truth: These situations cause us anxiety, and we have to deal with them eventually. Why not now?

Kelly, for example, knew she had serious dental work to be done. She was missing some teeth and her remaining teeth were beginning to shift. It was important for her health that she get bridges, as soon as possible. But Kelly was terrified of going to the dentist. She was afraid of the pain. She was afraid of not being in control. She was afraid of someone putting hands into her mouth. She was afraid of the injections. Kelly had managed to avoid the dental work for three years. Every day when she brushed her teeth, she experienced the anxiety of knowing that she had to either take care of her teeth or risk losing others. She talked to friends about it, even got to the point of making dental appointments but canceled them.

Finally Kelly met socially a dentist whom she trusted. She got to know him and grew to like him. Eventually he convinced her to have the corrective work done. She was able, at this point, with the trust she had developed in him, to go to the first visit. She was pleasantly surprised at how much less terrifying it was than she had imagined and even more delighted with the fact that she was much less anxious each time she brushed her teeth.

In a couple of months, when all the work was finished, Kelly's mouth looked terrific and she felt distinctly relieved.

Each one of us probably has at least one unpleasant task hanging over our heads, accompanied with anxiety and perhaps guilt. This week choose one of these tasks. Spend the first three days thinking about why you have avoided it, what causes you anxiety about it, and how you could most comfortably deal with it. Would it be easier for you, for example, to go to the doctor if a relative or friend went with you? Would it help you to get a professional to do your taxes? Could someone help you finish that work assignment, even if they are there mostly for moral support? Would you be more likely to make that confrontation if you promised yourself a reward afterward? Find the way that you can reach your goal with the least discomfort.

During the last four days, make and execute a plan that

will take care of the task. This could be making a doctor's or accountant's appointment and getting things in order for the appointment, setting a time to do that assignment or make that confrontation, or any other way you can resolve the anxiety-filled situation.

Anxiety saps your energy and increases stress. Do yourself a favor this week. Face an anxiety.

I claim my true authority.

We are all knowledgeable in our own areas. We all know more than anyone else about ourselves. And yet at times we abdicate our authority and give it to someone else, even when it is not the right thing to do.

There are many reasons we do this. We may want the approval of the other and fear angering her or him by disagreeing. We may feel unwilling to deal with the feelings arising from a confrontation, and so choose to let things go. We may want to feel that the other person can take care of us, and may not want to see that we are equally able. The other person may be in a position of power over us and we don't want to anger them.

In all these cases, the end result is that we sell out our true authority for some other "gain." The stress it places on us is a feeling that we ourselves don't have what it takes to make our own decisions, and an accompanying feeling of dependency on outside authority. Along with this comes a fear and anger at the outside authority for the power he or she has over us.

Claiming our true authority is freeing. It frees us to make our own decisions. It frees us from the feelings of dependency, fear, and anger toward outside authorities. And it frees our creative energies to move forward.

It is amazing to notice in how many small ways we are willing to give over our inner authority. We listen to people who tell us what is best for us to eat rather than listening to our own bodies. We listen to advice from others about our relationships rather than sensing from inside of ourselves what we need to do. We change our minds about life choices because we let our self-doubt be reinforced by others.

Yes, of course there are times when it is advisable to change our minds. But there are others when we do it because we are feeling insecure.

This week we will observe how much we abdicate our inner authority, and start to practice asserting it.

For the first three days, notice how many times another person influenced you to change your mind. Which of these times did you change to a more truthful position? And which of these times did you desert the truth as you saw it? Did you find yourself changing your mind more often when you saw the other person as an authority? Did you find yourself asserting your point of view more strongly when you saw yourself more as the authority? Did you change your position more often when you spoke with a man? A woman? Someone close to you? Did you sometimes feign agreement with another when you really didn't mean it? Did you leave conversations wondering, "Why did I say that?"

Use these few days to get a sense of how you use your authority. Are you courageous or cowardly? Do you feel more comfortable claiming your authority or negating it? Do you feel more or less stressed when you are feeling authoritative?

For the last four days, practice asserting your authority. If you notice that you are changing your mind, stop for a few seconds and ask yourself, "Wait a minute. What is the truth here? What do I really believe about this?" Then re-state your true belief.

Claim your true authority this week. You'll enjoy the freedom.

I pace myself and vary my activities.

Each one of us is unique, with our own pacing, rhythms, and styles. Some of us are morning people, waking up easily and ready to go. Others of us are night people, sluggish in the morning and full of energy at night. Some of us work better with a tight schedule, and others of us like the freedom of a loose structure. Some of us function better with large blocks of productive time, and others work better with small units of time and frequent breaks.

No style is better than another. They are just different. Stress is caused when we are not aware of our particular style and we try to fit outselves into a different mold. Then we are working against our own grain. We are trying to make ourselves into someone we are not.

Oftimes as we were growing up, we were taught that one style was better than another. We believed it and perhaps felt guilty because we didn't follow it. We may even still feel guilty if we aren't "early to bed, early to rise" people, and we may blame our sleep rhythms for the fact that we aren't "healthy, wealthy, and wise."

What is more gratifying, however, is to learn how each one of us functions best. By knowing this and honoring our own personal rhythms and styles, we can be less stressed and more productive.

For the first two days this week, observe and identify your own personal rhythms. How much sleep is best for you? Six, seven, or eight hours continuously or perhaps five straight hours and a two-hour nap at another time or some other combination. (Thomas Edison, we are told, took only catnaps.) Do you need three regular meals a day, or do you function better if you have six small ones or two large ones, or simply eating when you're hungry? Do you do mental work better in the morning, afternoon, or evening? Are you sharper if you take breaks every hour or every half hour? Do you do better taking an exercise break, a snack break, or a relaxation break? When are your low-energy periods? (Late afternoon, for example, is a common low-energy period.) What helps you recharge? How can you arrange your responsibilities so that there is variety and coordination with your personal needs and rhythms? Is there something you do that saps your energy? (Watching TV is an example for some people. Eating sugar is another.)

For the next two days, observe whether you live your life in harmony with your own rhythms and your own need for variety. Do you have a way of dealing with your low-energy points? Can you regain your concentration when it strays? Can you alternate activities so that you don't get burned-out? Are you happy with your eating and sleeping schedules? Can you do your most difficult work when you are most alert and your least demanding when you are most tired? Can you rest and take breaks when you need to?

On the fifth day, list what changes you would like to make to live more harmoniously with your personal rhythms.

For the last two days, implement three of these changes. Notice how you feel as you make the changes. Do the changes enhance your day or detract from it? Do you have more energy or less? Are you more productive or less productive?

Pace yourself and vary your activities this week. You'll profit by it!

I weigh the risks I take.

Life is filled with risks. Each time we walk down a street, ride in a car, talk to a stranger, or try something new, we are taking a risk. Risks are important and essential in our lives. They add excitement, and are often associated with opportunity. There are, however, risks disproportionate to the gain, which increase stress with little reward.

It is these stressful, nonproductive risks that we will observe this week. At one time or another, all of us probably have taken careless risks. They are motivated by a need for excitement, impulsiveness, self-destructiveness, anger, and irrational emotions. They give us a feeling of anxiety or excitement.

One of the most common examples of risk with little gain is race car driving on the highway. Race car driving is driving to get somewhere as if you were in a race, passing every car in front of you, zigzagging in and out, and acting as if you had to get to your destination immediately. The driver often derives a sense of power from this type of driving but rarely decreases his or her driving time significantly. The risk of accident is high, and the chance of a real award—getting somewhere much sooner than if one drove safely—is practically nonexistent. In addition, the driver and the riders feel anxious, putting unnecessary stress on themselves.

This type of risk is simply not worth the stress. Safe driving, within the speed limit, may not feel as exciting but is more likely to get you where you're going unscathed.

Gambling is an example of a risk that can be either productive or self-destructive. Gambling can be very exciting and profitable if done well and thoughtfully. Business ventures and stock investments are both gambles, but if they are well thought-out and accompanied by a little luck, both can be profitable.

Casino gambling, on the other hand, is less likely to be profitable. Certainly, it can be occasionally, but casinos wouldn't stay in business if this were the rule. Casinos are in business because gambling is more profitable for them than for the gamblers. So investing money in casino games can pay off in fun, but don't expect it to be profitable.

The most important thing about taking risks is knowing why you are taking them and what the potential payoff and price are. There may be nothing wrong with gambling in a casino if you are realistic about your chances of winning and if you can afford what you lose. It could provide a lot of fun.

For some people, however, casino gambling is disastrous. These people lose all perspective and lose touch with the price they're paying for the excitement. Compulsive gamblers can lose their lives' savings without being able to stop.

What becomes obvious here is that risks are important, and can be fun and profitable, but we need to know what we are risking and for what reason.

This week for the first two days, observe yourself in relation to risks. Do you take many risks? Are you conservative and calm? Do you lead a low-risk life, or do you have disdain for caution and take lots of big risks? Do you have a sense of balance about the risks you take? Are they reasonable and profitable? Get to know your style of risk taking.

For the next two days, think about your risk-taking style. Does it fit you? Are you comfortable with it? Does it leave you frustrated or fulfilled? Are you stressed by it? Is it exciting enough for you? Do you benefit enough from it? Do you yearn to take more risks? Do you need to temper your risks? Do you take material risks and avoid interpersonal risks? Or vice versa?

On the fifth day, if you've found you don't like the way you handle risks, make a plan to alter your style of risk taking. Be specific about where you need to change your habits. You may need to take risks to ask people for what you need and take fewer risks in your driving. Or you may need to take more financial risks and expose fewer vulnerabilities to acquaintances.

For the last two days, implement three changes in risk taking you have decided upon. Be conscious of how you feel as you change your former habits. Does it feel better and less stressful to you? Do you like it better now, or was it better for you before?

Weigh your risks this week. You'll feel more secure for it.

I am truthful.

Polygraph machines demonstrate the stress of being un-truthful: Changes reflective of the fight or flight response. Yet we all add this stress to our lives in varying amounts. We are untruthful to ourselves, to those close to us, and to others. We are untruthful in small ways, and we tell whop-ping lies. Sometimes we know it, and sometimes we don't. We usually do it to protect ourselves in some way.

We lie to protect ourselves from the truth, and we lie to get our own way. We lie to protect ourselves from some-one's anger, and we lie to save face. Sometimes we don't even realize we are lying, because we are lying to our-selves as well. We lie for many reasons. Each time we lie, we add stress to our lives.

It is difficult to be truthful all the time. It takes diligence and attention. We have habitual responses that don't always reflect the truth. For example, "How's business?" is often answered unthinkingly with a "Fine, thanks" when "It's great" or "Not so good" would be more accurate.

We have fears that keep us from being truthful. We are afraid that people will be angry with us, dislike us, leave us, if we tell them truths they don't want to hear. We have a social consciousness and a sensitivity to others' feelings that make it difficult to be honest. There are those we need on our side with whom we are afraid to be honest.

Self-delusion, however, is by far the most insidious kind of untruthfulness. It keeps us from knowing the truth about ourselves and makes us operate on a level of unreality, preventing us from participating fully in our lives. The result is self-alienation.

This week we are going to become more conscious about how truthful we are with ourselves and others and spend some time practicing being more truthful.

For the first three days, listen to yourself as you speak with others. How truthful are you? Do you use white lies? Do you tell whoppers? Do you exaggerate? How do you feel when you listen to yourself when you are untruthful? Do you feel at ease? Uncomfortable? Guilty? Scared?

For the last four days, catch yourself in at least two untruths each day and correct them. Face the feelings you may have about correcting them. Accept yourself and your feelings. Give yourself credit for your courage in telling the truth. Realize that you are relieving stress and building self-esteem and integrity.

Be truthful this week. You deserve it.

I monitor my exposure
to environmental
stress.

We are all subject to stress arising from conditions outside of us. Stress from the environment is created in many ways: noise, polluted air, uncomfortable temperature, unpleasant humidity, toxins, dirt, clutter, uncomfortable furniture, poor lighting, radiation from appliances (computers, TVs, microwave ovens), uncomfortable clothes, and inadequate privacy. At any given time we're usually dealing with some environmental stress. It's inevitable.

The consequences of these stresses are varied, and yet ultimately, each one decreases our available energy. We struggle to concentrate against a background of noise. Our bodies must filter out and process the toxins in air pollution. We strive for homeostasis in hot, cold, humid, and dry conditions. Our minds look for organization amid clutter. We strain to see in poor lighting. We lose energy and health from radiation. We turn off our senses to uncomfortable clothes. And we seek isolation for privacy.

Yet by becoming aware of these stresses in our lives, we can minimize and, in some cases, even eliminate them. This is a special challenge for those of us who live in cities, but with a bit of effort, it can be done.

This week we will pay attention to these environmental

stresses and put some effort into decreasing them. For the first three days, pay attention to how you feel at home, work, traveling, outside, wherever you may be. Listen, smell, sense how the environment feels to you. Is it noisy? Polluted? Or is it quiet and clean? Are the temperature and humidity comfortable? Is there enough humidity so that your nose and mouth remain moist? Are things neat and organized or cluttered and chaotic? How does your mind react to the neatness or clutter? Is the lighting adequate so that you can see easily? Are fluorescent lights used? Some people become tired from fluorescent lighting—do you? Do you limit exposure to radiation from TV and computer terminals? Are your clothes as comfortable as they could be? Do they breathe? Are they roomy enough to be comfortable? Does your furniture support you and fit you? Do you have enough privacy that you don't feel encroached upon?

By answering these questions, you will become more conscious of your environment and how it affects you. This will give you a direction for the last four days' exercise.

For the last four days, decide which of the environmental stresses bothers you the most, and decrease one stressful condition each day. So choose four conditions that really bother you, and think of ways to decrease them. For example, if it's winter and you're in a cold climate in which the heating system decreases the relative humidity to the point that your nose and mouth are dry, humidify the air with a steamer or humidifier. If your clothes are too tight, loosen them. Unbutton a button right now if you have to. You'll feel the difference immediately.

Of course, some conditions are simply out of our control. Acknowledging this is helpful in reducing the stress they cause, as we can stop fighting them as if we could change them.

Decrease some environmental stress this week. You'll feel more at home in your environment.

I empower myself by taking responsibility.

☐

Empowering ourselves by taking responsibility in situations is a great way to reduce stress. Time and again we see that stress is caused by situations in which we feel we have no control. Studies conclude that the feeling of being able to control the outcome of the situation is essential to reducing stress. Yet many of us abdicate power in our lives by denying self-responsibility.

The willingness to take responsibility has the opposite effect: We feel in charge and able to make change. But being in charge can be scary. This means that we cannot blame the state of our lives on other people or outside circumstances. It means that we ourselves have conceived and created the situations in our lives, and it means that we have responsibility for both what we're pleased with and what we would like to change.

We all have ways of avoiding self-responsibility and thus losing our sense of being in charge. We do it when we deny our part in creating an argument. ("I wouldn't have yelled if John hadn't said that I'm not doing a good job." Instead of, "I really got angry at John when he said I'm not doing a good job. I wish I could have just told him how it made me feel.")

We also do it when we make excuses for our mistakes. ("I wouldn't have hit the car in front of me if he hadn't stopped short without warning," instead of "I really was following the car too closely to stop quickly if I had to.")

We abdicate self-responsibility when we think of ourselves as being a victim of someone else instead of seeing our part; for example, "My lousy old boss just fired me," instead of "I just got fired because I've been late every day for the last two years."

We surrender responsibility when we blame others. "I could enjoy sex much more if my spouse were a better lover," instead of "My spouse and I really need to communicate better to each other about our sexual needs."

The perspective of self-responsibility in our lives is very powerful. It helps us see reality more clearly. It enables us to be more active and effective in creating what we want. It facilitates making changes to modify what we don't like. It is optimistic and hopeful. And it can relieve the stress of not feeling in charge.

This week we are going to learn to empower ourselves by taking responsibility.

Choose an area of your life in which you habitually avoid responsibility. Examine it from the point of view that you may have an effect on it that you don't see. Look for any way you may have an effect: secret pleasure you may derive from the status quo; avoiding possible action; avoiding influencing another who could effect change; escape from responsibility by not involving yourself; saving face by denying your part.

If you discover that you are guilty in one of the above ways, take action to change it. You may need to change an attitude, speak to someone, or change the situation yourself.

If after doing the above exercise, you still do not see your part in the situation, create an affirmation to change it—for example, I am a strong and loving human being, and I see my part in the situation. (For directions, see the exercise in "I Use Affirmations to Change My Life.")

Take time to imagine yourself taking responsibility. Re-create the situation step by step so that you see exactly how you are responsible. Feel the new reality with all your senses: See, touch, taste, smell, and hear in your imagination yourself being responsible. How does it affect you emotionally? Often in our lives we avoid responsibility because we are secretly afraid of success. We may fear that we can't replicate the success, that others will be jealous and dislike us, or that we may prove to be more effective than those to whom we look for reassurance and guidance. We may also have fears of competition.

Acknowledge and accept these fears if you have them, and continue daily to do the affirmation and imagination exercises. Keep alert to the situation and observe whether you take responsibility for your part more readily. This may or may not happen in one week of concentrated effort. You may want to continue this exercise for an extended time period in order to effect a change.

Take responsibility this week. It will empower you!

I can work through a phobia.

Each one of us is confronted with fear at some time. We may be afraid of concrete situations, such as being bitten by a dog, being fired by our boss, falling from a high place, losing someone we care about, or even speaking to strangers. Or we may have general fears, like being afraid of the unknown.

We know how it feels to have fear. Dry mouth, perspiration, pounding heart, nausea, butterflies in the stomach, lump in the throat, urge to urinate, tightness in the chest, empty feeling in the pit of the stomach, headache, restlessness, desire to move around, and a sense of impending doom are all symptomatic of fear. We each have a particular set of feelings that for us indicates fear, and we all share some in common.

Unconfronted fears become stressful. If you do not deal with the fear, it becomes chronic and sometimes develops into a fear of the fear itself. So now you have double jeopardy: the fear and fear of the fear.

An effective way to reduce this stress is to face and reduce the fear. It takes courage and dedication, but it can be managed.

This week choose one fear to face. Once you have chosen a fear, use the following three techniques to help you reduce your fear: desensitization, affirmation, and relaxation. The affirmation technique is to reeducate your mind and belief system about the truth of the situation. Find as many misconceptions you have about the fear as possible, and write the opposite—the truth—in the present tense on a small notecard. For example, someone afraid of flying might write, flying is safe, or I am safer flying than in my car. (Refer to earlier week, "I use affirmations to change my life," for the details of using affirmations.)

Use the breathing relaxation technique when you are actually in a fear-producing situation. This is not always possible, but when it is, it is helpful. Focus all your attention onto observing your breathing and counting your breaths from one to four. When you reach the fifth breath, start again with number one. When your mind wanders to a fearful thought, gently let the thought go and bring your mind back to the counting.

It is best to do the desensitization technique with a trusted friend. Imagine the fearful situation. Fill in the details of the sights, sounds, smells, sensations, and tastes associated with it. See yourself going through it from beginning to end with a positive outcome. Express your fears and anxieties to your friend. Ask your friend to comfort and reassure you. Allow yourself to know that this experience is representative of the real thing and that you have traversed it safely.

At the end of this week, your fear level should have lessened and your stress reduced.

Take your courage in hand. Face a fear.

I stay in the present.

Staying in the present, or staying in the now, is a key to reducing stress. It does so by keeping you focused in the area of your life where you can be most effective: the now. If you want to change something right now, it is possible. And you won't end up frustrated by wishing and regretting.

It is enlightening to realize how much time is spent thinking about the past and the future rather than the present. For the most part, the past is done and cannot be changed and the future is unknown. We can plan for it and have hopes for it, but we can't control it. The only part of our life that we can truly effect is the present.

There are different styles of avoiding the now. Some of us are most often in the future, daydreaming about how things could be. Others of us look back and think about how different things would be "if only I had done" something else. The more we focus our attention on the past and the future, the less we are in the now.

Marianne is an example of the latter. She is now forty, single, and in a dead-end position in a large company, despite the fact that she is capable and intelligent. She is greatly frustrated with her life. She looks back and says things like "If I only had studied business in college, I would be ahead now. If only I had taken that other job, I would be making more now. I wish I had spent more time promoting my social life. I might have been married by now."

The result is that Marianne comes across to people as a discouraged, disheartened woman. This limits her chances of success. More important, however, is the fact that this attitude undermines Marianne's own efforts to make headway toward her goals. If Marianne would take each statement about the past and put it in the present tense, she would have something real to work with.

For example, she could say, "I can study business now." "I can look for a better job now." "I can concentrate on my social life now." Each of these statements can lead to changes in Marianne's life, and that is what she really wants. The statements in the now create opportunities and a direction for her. And, most important, they offer a hope of fulfillment.

This week spend the first three days observing your own relationship to the present. Are you usually concerned with what is happening in the moment, or are you letting the world go by as you think about the past and future? Do you fill yourself with disappointments and regrets about the past? False hopes about the future? Or are you fully in the present, taking charge of your life in the now?

For the last four days, notice when you are out of the present at least twice a day. At that moment, bring yourself to the present and take charge of yourself in the now.

Often we leave the present when we feel threatened, so it may be a bit difficult to bring yourself back. That's okay. Being aware of this will initiate a change of attitude. Be gentle with yourself. These are long-established habits, and they will probably resist change. Don't force. Simply observe when you resist coming back to the now. Gradually you will find yourself spending more and more time in the present.

Give yourself a present. Stay in the *now*.

I make myself a priority.

Many of us feel we have too little time and too much to do. The feeling of being overscheduled is stressful. It seems as if we can't take time for ourselves until we complete all our duties. Eventually we feel burned-out. It is frustrating to feel that there is always more to do, that you are never finished. And it's even more frustrating to feel you don't deserve free time because there are more responsibilities.

Many of us feel heroic by being overscheduled. This can make us feel important. This feeling, however, can be the first step to burnout. Burnout occurs when you lose interest and effectiveness in your work (a job, schoolwork, home and family work) because it has come to dominate your life.

Jayne is an example of someone headed for burnout. She works full-time as a designer, is married, with two small children, and is responsible for running a large home. She is feeling overscheduled.

Jayne's typical day begins at 5:00 A.M. as she attends to preparing herself for work. She then washes and dresses the children and prepares breakfast for the family. After cleaning up breakfast, she packs the kids in the car, drops them at their respective schools, and heads for work. She leaves work at 3:00 to take the children to child care, goes back to work, and arrives home again at 5:30, just in time to prepare dinner and set the table. After cleaning up the dinner dishes, she bathes and dresses the kids for bed, reads them their stories individually, and puts them to bed. It is now about 9:00. By this time she is exhausted and wants some time for herself, but it is also the only time she has to spend with her husband.

Weekends are occupied with food shopping, clothes washing and ironing, mending, paying bills, house maintenance, socializing, and church. Jayne has not allowed any time for herself.

Jayne is beginning to feel resentful and angry. When anyone asks her to do something for him or her, she snaps at the person. She yells at the children more and more, and things between her and her husband are becoming rocky. In addition, she has been having chronic abdominal pains, which have been diagnosed as the beginning of colitis, an irritated colon.

Jayne is in a difficult situation. She is doing what she believes is best for everyone, giving to them and her job with every minute she has. And yet her self-sacrificing is extracting a great price: Her peace of mind and physical health as well as family harmony.

This could all change if Jayne would only believe that her needs are as important or even more important than others' needs. In order to balance her needs with those of her family and her job, Jayne needs to do the following: Get help with the children and the home; reevaluate the amount of time she spends at work; enlist more understanding and cooperation from her husband.

How high a priority are your personal needs? Do you give yourself enough time for yourself? Do you take care of the essentials—food, sleep, and exercise? Do you have time for family fun and socializing? Do you have time for pure fun? Can you give in to your "frivolous" desires?

This week spend two days evaluating your habits in relation to your own needs. How much time each day do you take for yourself? What percentage of your waking day is that? Does that seem like enough to you? Do you need and deserve more?

For the other five days, decide how much time you want to give entirely to yourself for pleasure and needs. You can use it to do things by yourself or with others. It can be time for reading, doing relaxation exercises, singing, playing music, sports, bathing luxuriously, being taken care of in some way, going to a restaurant, seeing a movie, going dancing, or whatever it is that is missing from your life that you truly want to do. The important thing is that each day, you make room for yourself and the things that you want to do just for you.

Don't worry about becoming self-indulgent. You will find a balance between too much time for yourself and not enough. And you will find that you are feeling happier and more satisfied with your life. You deserve to be the highest priority in your life. No one else will do it for you. Avoid burnout—make yourself a priority.

I let go of a frustration.

What is frustration? It is an area in our life in which we feel thwarted, in which we feel we will never attain our goal. Frustration produces stress by making us feel we are pushing against a brick wall. We often react to frustration by getting angry, which only complicates the situation. The most stressful part of frustration is feeling powerless.

Sometimes we feel powerless when we actually are not. There are avenues of action open to us that we have not seen or considered. For example, imagine that you are working against a deadline to complete a project. You are being bothered by all sorts of interruptions: telephone calls, family members, associates. You go along with the interruptions for a while—and then the next time one comes along, you blow up. Enough. You are being frustrated in your attempt to complete your job. And yet you feel anxious in ignoring the telephone, mean in ignoring your family, and anti-social in ignoring your associates.

It is possible to take the phone off the hook and make it clear to others not to disturb you without being mean and antisocial. People will understand if you explain clearly why you cannot be disturbed. The frustration created by the interruptions has been eliminated.

Other times the only way to deal with the frustration is to alter our goals.

Imagine being caught in traffic on the way to a special event. You've been looking forward to this evening for a long time, and now it's finally arrived, and here you are sitting in traffic rather than having the time of your life. Time passes. Your thoughts go from the party to the traffic and back to the party again. The more you think about what you're missing, the more frustrated you become. Finally, by the time the traffic is moving again, you're so frustrated and angry you're not fit to spend time with either man or beast.

In a different scenario, you're stuck in traffic on the way to the same event but decide to use this time to yourself to help prepare to enjoy the evening. You begin to say an affirmation to insure that you feel open and friendly during the party. Your anticipation rises as you actually experience yourself meeting and enjoying new people. Your goals have now changed: Simply arriving at the party on time has changed to arriving at the party safe and in an open and friendly mood. Your frustration has been relieved by adapting your goals, and you don't generate unnecessary anger.

How often do you get caught up in frustration? In modern society frustration is constantly with us: getting stuck in traffic; trying to juggle the responsibilities of many roles; expecting people to keep their word when they won't; trying to get a machine to work when it's broken; having something repaired correctly the first time. The list goes on and on. What are yours?

This week spend some time identifying your most annoying frustrations. They may be with family or friends, colleagues or bosses, machines or things. Whatever they are, list them and decide how and why they annoy you. Then—and this is the crucial step in determining what to do—decide whether there is truly anything you can do about it. Is there any way you can change the situation, or are you going to have to change your goal to relieve the frustration?

At this point, take one frustration that is important to you, and decide to change it. Decide whether you can change the situation, or have to change your goal. Then outline a plan of action for yourself, taking steps either to change the frustration or to change your goal. Next put the plan into effect.

How does it feel? People often report feeling relieved and lighter. Their minds seem clearer and decisions seem to come more easily. How does it feel to you?

Give up a few frustrations this week. It's a sacrifice you can't afford to be without.

I let myself be taken care of.

In this mad, fast-moving world we live in, we often forget to allow moments for ourselves to feel taken care of. We become enamored of the image of ourselves as competent, effective adults and forget that inside each of us there still lives a small child who needs attention and care.

The idea of letting someone else take care of us for a while may be uncomfortable for some of us. It means giving over control, letting go responsibility, even being passive. This can elicit feelings of anxiety, especially for people who identify themselves as take charge types.

It is important, however, to overcome these feelings of anxiety and give in to the inner child's needs to be cared for. It doesn't have to be a total surrender, just some small way of acknowledging these needs and indulging yourself in some care.

For example, you can go to a salon and have your hair done or have a facial or manicure. You can find a good masseur or masseuse and have a massage. You can take yourself out to a restaurant and have your favorite meal. You can have your shoes shined. You can ask a friend to read you a story and tuck you in to bed at night. You can hire a driver and a car to drive you around instead of driving yourself. You can ask someone to bathe you in a sudsy bubble bath.

You know best what you need in order to feel taken care of. This week let yourself be taken care of at least three times in different ways. It doesn't have to be in big ways, but it does require you asking someone to do something for you that you ordinarily would do for yourself.

Listen for the voice of your inner child. Think back to your childhood and remember what you wanted or enjoyed at that time. Pay attention to what makes you feel the most loved now. Use these cues to help you decide what kind of taking care of you need the most. Then go out and get it. Let yourself feel taken care of in the way you most want to be.

Be good to your inner child this week. Let yourself be taken care of.

I can confront
someone gently.

Each one of us has unfinished business with someone resulting from unresolved feelings. Carrying this burden around is stressful.

Unresolved feelings toward someone block communication. We feel awkward when we speak to him. We may even feel distanced from him. Our mind may play tricks on us, giving us irrational reasons to stay away from that person. We may allow ourselves to remember only the negative aspects of the relationship. The closer this person is to us and the more important he or she is in our lives, the more stressful this becomes.

It takes an act of courage on our part to broach a touchy subject. The confrontations we need to make are often about times when we hurt or offend each other, and it is rare that we can talk easily about them.

Often confrontations reveal simple, underlying misunderstandings: Things said earlier that have been forgotten or changed, a third person conveying misinformation or misheard information. These are the easiest conflicts to resolve. Once the misunderstanding is uncovered, most people find it easy to forgive and feel good about each other again.

More difficult to resolve are confrontations in which someone has actually done something hurtful. In these cases we need to deal with feelings of pride, fear, embarrassment, anger, hurt, and humiliation. It is important to remember that as uncomfortable as each of those feelings is, we can experience them and survive well. Actually, we can experience them and be stronger for our effort.

This week we are going to confront someone and attempt to resolve the feelings involved.

For the first two days, think of someone you have been avoiding because of unresolved feelings. It could be a relative, friend, business associate, or neighbor.

For these two days, think about the incident that created the feelings. It could have been something as small as a thoughtlessly spoken word to something as large as a fraudulent business transaction or a personal betrayal. Try to recreate the situation in your mind and understand it as best you can from both sides. See if you can determine what went wrong and why.

For the next two days, imagine yourself speaking to the other person involved. What do you say? How does he respond? How do you react? How do you feel? How do you deal with his feelings? Your feelings? Does the conversation escalate into a heated discussion or stay cool?

For the next two days, make an arrangement to meet with the other person or, if that is not possible, to speak on the phone with him. Organize your thoughts about the incident. Know what you want to say to the other person, avoiding blaming and name-calling.

Finally meet with or telephone the person and try to resolve the feelings involved. Take responsibility for your actions and reactions. Avoid blaming. If you have a feeling, it is yours, and even if it is only a reaction to the other person, you still have a right to your feelings. Speak with the person as gently and evenly as you can, expressing how you were affected by the event. Listen to the other person's explanation or viewpoint. Try to understand it, even if you disagree with it.

Find a way, if you can, to forgive, even if you're not forgiven. Find a way to care, even if you don't feel cared for. See if you can feel good about the other person even if they don't feel good about you. It is you who will be freed from the burden of carrying unresolved feelings.

In the best possible case, both parties will understand, forgive, and feel good about themselves and each other. If this occurs, congratulations. You're both freer and probably feel better than ever about each other.

Confront someone gently this week. Free yourself from unresolved feelings.

I use word power to relieve stress.

□

Words have a lot of power. They influence the way we think and feel. To demonstrate, try this exercise.

Say to yourself that tomorrow is going to be a great day. You are going to awaken feeling well, with lots of energy. You are going to tackle all your responsibilities with gusto and zeal. Things are going to go right for you, and you will have a fulfilling, fun, and productive day.

How do you feel? Most people will feel positive and uplifted after saying these things to themselves.

Now try the opposite. Tell yourself that tomorrow you will wake up slowly and feel very heavy. You will have to force yourself out of bed. Gradually you will face the tasks of the day feeling overloaded and overwhelmed. Things will not go smoothly. Everything will be complicated and will take extra time and trouble. You will be grouchy and will fight with everyone. The day will be interminable, and you will finally fall into bed exhausted and disheartened.

Now how do you feel? This usually leaves people feeling low and letdown. Clearly, the quality of our inner dialogue influences the amount of stress we experience.

It is important to realize that we talk to ourselves much of the time even if we are not conscious of it. We cannot perhaps control the unconscious talk, but we can control the conscious talk. It is obvious from the above demonstration that how we talk to ourselves influences how we feel. Using this knowledge, we can consciously attempt to talk to ourselves in an honest, balanced way.

This week we are going to practice speaking to ourselves with an awareness that words have power.

For the first three days, simply observe the chatter in your mind. Be aware of it. Listen to it. Is it positive or negative? Is it truthful or deceptive? Is it balanced or exaggerated? Is it calm or hysterical? Is it accepting or denying? How do you feel when you listen to it?

It is important that you let the chatter be there, whatever it is. Let it be, acknowledging its content and your reaction to it.

For the last four days, choose one negative mental conversation each day and actively enter into it, making it more positive and truthful.

For example, you may be preparing for an important meeting when you hear yourself saying, "I know I'm going to mess this up. I'll never get my hair to look right. My boss is going to hate my presentation. He's probably going to fire me."

You can correct this by saying, "I've done the work. My clothes look all right. I believe in what I'm saying. I can deliver my presentation calmly."

How does it feel being more positive? More precise? Do you feel more in control and thus less stressed? Do you recognize how you influence your emotional state in this way?

Use the power of words in your favor this week. You deserve it.

I make sure to get enough sleep.

□

Do you get enough sleep? How do you know whether you're getting enough sleep? Do you wake up naturally or with an alarm clock? If you could sleep as long as you liked, how long would you sleep? Do you feel like you need more sleep? Are you able to sleep in the time allotted to sleeping, or are you sometimes too anxious to sleep at that time? Each day feel when you wake up, record your sleeping patterns, and after a week, review them and decide whether you are partaking enough of this renewing experience called sleep.

If you are, great. If you're not, ask yourself how you can change your habits so that there is enough time for you to sleep fully. Care enough about yourself to make the changes that will afford you more sleep and rest. You may be able to work a nap into your day. You may find ways to decrease your need for sleep by exercising, changing your diet, or taking relaxation periods during the day. You may also decide you have to eliminate some activities to make more time for sleep.

Watching babies and young children sleep is a reminder that our bodies can tell us when we need to sleep—if we listen. Children can fall asleep almost anywhere. Even the loudest crowd won't bother them if they need to sleep. Pay attention to your own body's messages. Map out your sleeping patterns. You may need a nap at four o'clock in the afternoon but can't work it in. Could you do a five-minute relaxation exercise at four o'clock instead? This could be enough to recharge your system for a while.

Sleep is important and necessary for our physical and mental health. If you are shortchanging yourself of necessary rest, ask yourself why. Some people are tense if they are not doing something at all times. Is this true of you? Some people are afraid they'll miss out on something if they sleep. But think about what you might miss by not sleeping. During sleep your body processes slow down and your system rests. Your mind becomes occupied with the events of the past day and deals with some of your emotional issues. Sometimes during sleep, you are even able to solve problems or have new realizations.

Sleep needs are very personal, and you may need more or less sleep than other people. The trick is to get to know yourself well enough to determine how much sleep you need to function at your best. This week see how it feels to get the right amount of sleep. Remember that your sleep needs may change. Be attuned to how you feel when you're getting enough sleep, and use that as a barometer for planning your sleep and rest activities.

This week sleep well.

I let go of lost objects.

□

Is this a familiar scene? You're ready to go to work, and the last thing you check is whether you have your keys. They aren't in their usual place, and you start to search for them. You look in the next couple of places where you think they might be, and you start to feel your anxiety rise—it's getting later and later, and you still can't find them. The more tense you are, the more frantic and disorganized your search becomes and the later it gets. Finally you either find them or leave home without them. In any case, you've usually lost your sense of equilibrium and feel stressed.

These frantic searches are stressful and often avoidable. By some preplanning and letting go, we can either substitute with alternate sets of keys (or whatever it is that is essential to us) or allow ourselves to let go of whatever it is that we have lost. Much time and anxiety is spent in searching for lost items. Neither the time spent nor the peace sacrificed is replaceable.

Loss stimulates many associations that have little to do with the actual situation at hand. For example, it may not have been the keys in the above scenario that drove the search to such a frantic pace but rather the thought that "it

was so stupid of me to lose the keys" that motivated the
seeker to find them. It is usually these associations that
trigger the sense of panic or anxiety that accompanies losing an object. It is helpful to realize that the reactions we
are having to losing the object may be out of proportion to
the actual loss. This realization alone may be enough to
alleviate some of the anxiety.

This week pay attention to your reaction to losing
things. (If you don't lose anything this week, remember a
time when you did.) Do you take it easily, peacefully, or do
you get anxious and scared? Does it sit easily on your
mind, so you can let it go, or do you become obsessed with
finding it? Do you feel all right, or do you feel disturbed?
Notice whether losing things is stressful for you.

For the first four days, take stock of what you have that
would be terribly inconvenient for you to lose: keys, com-
binations to locks, beepers, important names and telephone
numbers, credit card numbers, insurance information, bank
information, bank books, checkbooks, stock and bond information, your will, and any other items that are important to you and your family. Once you have made this list,
duplicate anything that can be copied, and put the object
and its copy in different safe places. Make a list to remind
you where everything is, and put it in an obvious, safe
place. This removes the stress associated with finding
something right away if you're in a hurry. You simply substitute the copy.

For the next three days, practice letting go of some-
thing(s) you have lost. There is an old saying, "If you lose
something that is truly yours, it will come back to you. If it
doesn't, it wasn't truly yours." It may be difficult to part
with a piece of jewelry with sentimental value, or a valuable piece of equipment, and yet the damage of the stress
we put on ourselves may be much more significant to our
lives than the loss of the object itself.

If it is really essential to find what you have lost, you

can try a mental technique. Sit quietly counting your breaths in groups of four for ten minutes (1,2,3,4, 1,2,3,4, etc). Allow any intervening thoughts to burst like bubbles and disappear. Bring your mind back to counting your breaths. After ten minutes, with your eyes closed, see a blank screen, like a movie screen, in your mind's eye. Ask the question, "Where is my (glove)?" Wait and see what appears on the screen. Often you will see an image of where the lost object is.

Letting go of the loss involves accepting the loss and not dwelling on finding it. If the mental technique isn't fruitful, you may not find what you have lost. But it certainly doesn't warrant more of your time and energy worrying about it. If you find yourself constantly thinking about your loss, ask yourself what the loss means to you beyond the object itself. But most important, stop blaming yourself. Self-forgiveness is more constructive, and feels better, too.

Do an affirmation to help accept the loss: I am safe and healthy even without my (lost object). Try repeating the affirmation as often as you feel comfortable doing for seven days.

Let go of a lost object this week and let go of some stress.

I can relax by being in nature.

Each one of us has a deep need to be in contact with our inner nature. When we are surrounded by the trappings of modern life (cities, machines, noise, pollution), it is easy to begin to lose this connection. When it is lost, we become irritable, confused, undirected, and stressed.

It is sometimes necessary to redirect ourselves back to mother nature in order to preserve this invaluable connection with our own nature. There are unique qualities in natural things that affect us profoundly. The beauty of a flower; the calming effect of running water; the sensuality of rich, green grass; the transcendent azure of the sky; the gentle caressing of a zephyr; the mesmerizing quality of a fire; the solidity of an ancient mountain—they all help us reach into the depths of our own nature to renew and relax us.

Being in nature is relaxing for physiological reasons as well. Plants produce fresh oxygen and use carbon dioxide, thus supplying us with good, fresh air. Negative ions, which make us feel invigorated (for example, following an electrical storm) are also more plentiful in nature. By surrounding ourselves with a more nurturing environment, our bodies are able to relax and let down.

And certainly we are able to enhance our enjoyment of almost anything by simply being in nature. We are pleased to be able to relax sitting on a porch swing overlooking the ocean or to be able to see for miles around from the top of a mountain. We're happy to have a barbecue or go on a picnic. We look forward to going to the beach or a ride on a boat. And who can resist simply sitting in front of a fire on a frosty evening? We are so enriched by our contact with nature that it is surprising that we don't take the steps more often to provide ourselves with it.

This week make the effort to spend at least two solid hours in natural surroundings alone. If you are with others, go off somewhere by yourself. Tune into the environment: Listen, smell, touch, taste, and look. Concentrate on each sense individually. Let your thoughts slow down and disappear as you focus your attention totally on observing. Then sense into yourself. How do you respond to being alone in nature? Do you feel relaxed? Tense? Moved? Awed? Bored? Fascinated?

When you return home, ask yourself whether you want to bring more nature into your house. If so, do it in whatever way you enjoy most: shells, crystals, flowers, plants, animals. Bring into your home whatever helps you recapture the sense of the feelings you had when you were alone in nature.

Spend some time relaxing in nature this week. You'll be renewed by it.

I develop an appreciative perspective.

Seeing the world from an appreciative perspective is a way to relieve the stress of feeling unfulfilled and deprived. We all have our moments of truly understanding how much we have and of feeling fulfilled by that knowledge, but all too often we tend to concentrate on what we don't have—the lacks of our life. Focusing on what we don't have is necessary occasionally—when we are setting our goals and evaluating our progress—and yet it can be stressful and draining when it is our predominant world view.

To illustrate this idea, do a mental exercise. Look around you. Think about your place of work or your home. Focus on all the things that are lacking there, all the things that are on your Someday I'll Have list. List them mentally. Say them aloud. Say, "I don't have. . . ." Over and over, focus on what is missing that you would like to have. Then say, "I am really deprived because I don't have all that I want." Repeat that five times. How does this make you feel? Terrible, right?

Okay, now try the opposite. Think of all the things that you have that you really value and appreciate. Your family. Your friends. Your job. Your good feelings. Your health. Begin to list those saying, "I appreciate and am so grateful for. . . ." At the end say five times, "I am so fortunate and fulfilled because of all the wonderful things in my life." Now how do you feel. Great, right? And you're the same you with the same circumstances, just seen from a different perspective.

There really is no advantage to looking at the world from a perspective of deprivation. It does not feel good. It saps energy. It undermines forward movement. It creates a feeling of self-pity. It undermines our self-respect. In short, it feeds on itself and creates more deprivation.

Appreciation, in contrast, is creative. It feeds our energy, making us feel fulfilled and able to give more. It makes us feel upbeat, enthusiastic, and optimistic. We feel good about ourselves, our lives, and our abilities. From this foundation, we are able to go out and create more abundance in our lives.

This week we will pay attention to our particular world view. Then we will foster more appreciation in our viewpoint.

For the first three days, observe yourself. Do you tend to spend a lot of time wanting more and feeling deprived? Do you tend to find fault with what is available to you? Do you complain a lot? Or do you truly appreciate what is there? Do you express gratitude for even the simple things in your life such as food, shelter, loved ones? Do you acknowledge these things or take them for granted?

For the last four days of the week, catch yourself three times a day when you undermine your appreciation. In that moment first forgive yourself for your unappreciative attitude. Accept yourself with your limitations. Then change your viewpoint from one of deprecation to one of appreciation. Actually say the words that will change your attitude. If you find yourself complaining about your job, find a way to appreciate it. If you find yourself complaining about your lack of possessions, look around and appreciate what you do have. Remember that appreciating what you have does not mean you stop striving for improvement—it just means you do so with an attitude of fullness rather than with anger and empty deprivation.

How does this change of attitude affect you emotionally? Do you feel more positive more of the time? Does your life seem fuller? Do you feel happier?

Make the choice to give yourself more happiness by developing a more appreciative viewpoint.

I clean up unfinished business.

Most of us increase the stress in our lives by feeling that we are never finished with what we have to do. We contribute to this feeling by leaving things in our lives incomplete. We leave projects half-done, cleaning incomplete, correspondence unanswered and by so doing deprive ourselves of having the feeling of freedom from chores. This feeling of incompleteness encumbers us and saps our energy.

We can create a sense of completeness and freedom in our lives by taking care of all this unfinished business. It is surprising how little time and effort it does take to put things in order and complete them. So much energy can be devoted to procrastinating and rationalizing about why things can't be done, when the same energy could be devoted to the tasks at hand, completing them, and relieving us of their burden.

Look around you right now. How many things can you count within your line of vision that are still to be done? Are you aware of carrying them with you? Do they tug at you? Drag on you? Do they call to you? Annoy you visually? Do they in any way make you feel good? This week we are going to become aware of the unfinished things in our lives and the effect they have on us. Then we will finish some tasks and see how that feels.

For the first day, take stock of your life. Think of all the things that you have left incomplete in various areas: home, work, family, social, financial, and spiritual. Make a list of them for each area. Evaluate the lists and decide what is most important to deal with first.

For the next six days, spend one half hour a day devoted to completing things from the lists, in order of decreasing importance. Examples of things you might want to complete are organizing papers, drawers, and closets; making telephone calls; organizing photographs in albums; decorating; planning and organizing your wardrobe; fulfilling social obligations; completing correspondence; paying bills; and finishing projects and books you're reading (or writing).

Observe how you feel as you cross things off the list and see them finished. Does it feel satisfying and relieving? Do you feel freer to enjoy your leisure time? There may be things on your list that you decide not to complete. This is fine, too. The decision to let them go is another way of relieving you of their burden.

Simply making the lists, as you did on the first day, will relieve much of the stress associated with these incomplete areas. Actually completing them will take care of the rest.

Complete some unfinished business this week. You'll feel relieved by it.

Forgiveness can relieve stress.

Stress is created when we hold on to anger. We stimulate the physiological changes caused by anger, the fight or flight reaction, whenever we think about the person or situation that makes us angry. In addition, we are usually uncomfortable when we encounter someone we are angry at; as a result, we are stressed further by having to avoid them or by being uncomfortable when we are with them. Probably each one of us has at least one person with whom we are still angry for recent or past reasons.

This anger keeps us from being our most effective selves. By being in a state of anger, we expend energy, reduce our strength, and compromise our centeredness.

There is one very potent way to relieve the stress of this situation: forgiveness.

You can reach a state of forgiveness with or without the cooperation of the other person. The most satisfying resolution, of course, comes when the two of you talk the situation over and reach a common understanding in which you forgive each other. But since this won't always happen, we need a way to forgive even without the cooperation of the other person.

Here are some ways to help yourself forgive the other

person. First try to understand his or her point of view. You may need the help of a trusted friend to do this. Put yourself in the other's position, and see if you can empathize with his or her feelings. From this vantage point, you may be able to understand and forgive.

Another way to achieve forgiveness is to understand how you helped to create the situation. By truly recognizing and acknowledging your part in allowing the situation to develop, you can stop blaming the other person. You may have helped the situation to develop by provoking someone, trusting naively, not clarifying a contract, staying after you could have left, not taking the proper steps to protect yourself, misleading someone, speaking unclearly, not clarifying with the other what was heard, or making assumptions. There will certainly be times when your responsibility is not clear to you, but by seeking it, you will learn a great deal about yourself.

If methods one and two do not work well for you, then try simply letting go and forgiving directly. You will feel better if you forgive than if you stay angry. You can do this simply by acknowledging that we are all human, we all make mistakes, and we all hurt each other now and again. Acknowledging the other's humanity can help us forgive.

This week, identify one person you would like to forgive. It can be a family member, business associate, friend, lover, anyone with whom you are angry.

Then spend some time going over in your mind or with a trusted friend the situation that caused the anger. See exactly what made you angry. Did you feel discounted? Exploited? Hurt? Overlooked? Abused? Identify the feelings that contributed to your anger.

Now try to understand how the other person might be feeling. What did you say or do to that person that may have hurt or angered him or her? Does he or she feel abused or misunderstood?

Now try to see your responsibility or lack of it in creating the situation.

If by now you are still feeling angry and unforgiving, simply try to let go of the anger and forgive the other, for his or her humanness. Try using an affirmation: I forgive (name of person) (for reason), and I no longer feel angry. Repeat this affirmation as often as you feel comfortable doing every day for seven days.

Do not be dismayed if you now understand the situation better but still feel angry. Often the intellect runs ahead of the emotions and it takes a while for the anger to diminish, despite the fact that you see how you can forgive. Remember, to err is human, to forgive divine.

Know you have all to gain and nothing to lose by forgiving. Let go of some anger. Forgive someone this week.

Love is the ultimate stress reliever.

The love in our hearts, the love that makes us sing, the love in our spirit, is the best stress reducer of all.

On those days when we see beauty in a rain gutter, feel our hearts melt at the sight of a flower, and hold our arms open to everyone we see, we don't feel stressed. Our hearts and whole beings are open and flowing. We feel loving, positive, and powerful, and simultaneously peaceful and excited. We are exhilarated and energetic yet unstressed. We love ourselves, our loved ones, and our friends alike and even feel we can accept our enemies. We simply love and we love simply. On these days it's hard to get stressed.

Love is the opposite of fear, and fear underlies all stress. So it's easy to see that being in a state of love negates fear and stress.

To convince yourself, observe yourself the next time you feel a sustained experience of love. How do you react to the ordinary? Does it seem somehow more interesting and richer? How do you feel toward others? More tolerant, patient, and compassionate? How do you treat yourself? More gently? More considerately? More lovingly? Do you feel stressed, or do you feel at ease? Chances are you feel wonderful, get along with everyone, and have a wonderful day.

Love is the best gift you can give. It enhances everyone and everything. Our last assignment, to give love, is one you will need to practice over a lifetime. We need to keep love in mind each day of our lives and to believe that we are capable of giving and receiving love.

In order to do this, we need to remember that we have habits that keep us from loving. Through the exercises in this book we have discovered what triggers our anger and fear and we have learned ways of choosing alternate responses. We have the potential and the ability to be more loving, and to know that being more loving is being the best for ourselves and for others. This knowledge is the most powerful tool for stress reduction we can have. So let's begin to identify more with the love in our hearts than the fear in the pits of our stomachs.

By loving ourselves and spreading that love to others, we create the harmony and peace we all desire. It may be a bit threatening at first to put love into all we do; yet in it is our true security. Put more love into your life and the world. Remember, love is the ultimate stress reducer.

CATHERINE CIANCI KARAS received a B.S. in Physical Therapy from the College of Physicians and Surgeons, Columbia University. She has practiced physical therapy at the Gaylord Hospital in Wallingford, Connecticut; at New York University Medical Center (the Rusk Institute); Lenox Hill Hospital; and in conjunction with New York Hospital–Cornell Medical Center, New York City.

Ms. Karas received her M.A. in General Psychology and an Ed.M. in Vocational and Rehabilitation Counseling from Teachers College, Columbia University, in 1973. She then began a five-year study of Core Energetics, a psychotherapy that combines bodywork with analysis, at the Institute for the New Age. After graduation, she remained at the institute to teach anatomy and to supervise in the training program. During this time she was a leader of The Institute's Health Committee and gave many public talks and workshops on stress management. Ms. Karas has also lectured at New York University, Stony Brook University, the City College of New York, and Hunter College.

Ms. Karas has had a private practice in psychotherapy for the past eight years. Her continued interest in the interaction of mind and body has made stress the focus of her therapy work.

Ms. Karas is married and has a four-year-old daughter. She lives and practices in New York City.

By the year 2000, 2 out of 3 Americans could be illiterate.

It's true.

Today, 75 million adults...about one American in three, can't read adequately. And by the year 2000, U.S. News & World Report envisions an America with a literacy rate of only 30%.

Before that America comes to be, you can stop it...by joining the fight against illiteracy today.

Call the Coalition for Literacy at toll-free **1-800-228-8813** and volunteer.

Volunteer Against Illiteracy. The only degree you need is a degree of caring.

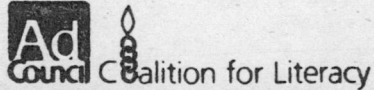

Ad Council Coalition for Literacy LV-2